POLICY ACTIONS FOR COVID-19 ECONOMIC RECOVERY

A COMPENDIUM OF POLICY BRIEFS
VOLUME 2

Edited by Ramesh Subramaniam, Alfredo Perdiguero, Jason Rush, and Pamela Asis-Layugan

JULY 2023

Contents

Figures

Figures

Foreword

The coronavirus disease (COVID-19) crisis resulted in lockdowns, border closures, and supply chain disruptions, significantly affecting lives and livelihoods across Southeast Asia and the globe. The pandemic's wide-ranging and long-term effects have highlighted the need for Southeast Asian countries to strengthen their resilience to future disruptions while reversing the damage brought about by COVID-19. As the pandemic wanes, efforts to revive economies sustainably are more critical than ever. There is a pressing need for post-pandemic policies and investments that lead to sustainable socioeconomic and environmental outcomes while enhancing economic resilience.

The Asian Development Bank (ADB) has provided enduring support to its developing member countries (DMCs) in mitigating the devastating social and economic impacts of COVID-19 and laying the groundwork for a more inclusive and resilient post-pandemic future. ADB convened the Policy Actions for COVID-19 Recovery (PACER) Dialogues to discuss cutting-edge knowledge and best practices that could help countries fast-track economic recovery and revival and foster regional cooperation to cushion the medium- and long-term effects of COVID-19.

This second compendium of policy briefs from the PACER Dialogues builds on the first compendium, highlighting recovery and revival strategies as the pandemic nears its end. Timely policy responses in vaccination and skills development, measures that can unleash the benefits of digitizing trade for greater efficiencies, and clean and green policies and investments are featured as policy actions that are vital to rebooting the global economy and ensuring low-carbon, inclusive, and climate-resilient recovery in the post-COVID-19 era. This compendium emphasizes the important role of regional cooperation and integration in countering the long-term effects of the COVID-19 crisis and strengthening solidarity among nations.

The ADB-sponsored PACER Dialogues held from February 2021 to July 2022 were supported under the framework of the Brunei Darussalam–Indonesia–Malaysia–Philippines East ASEAN Growth Area (BIMP-EAGA), the Indonesia–Malaysia–Thailand Growth Triangle (IMT-GT), and the Greater Mekong Subregion (GMS) Capacity Building Program or B-I-G Program.

We hope this second compendium will serve as a valuable resource for policy makers, development planners, and other stakeholders as they work toward mitigating the devastating effects of COVID-19 and in implementing pandemic-proof policy actions.

Ramesh Subramaniam
Director General and Chief, Sectors Group, Asia and the Pacific
Asian Development Bank

Abbreviations

4IR	Fourth Industrial Revolution
ACGF	ASEAN Catalytic Green Finance Facility
ADB	Asian Development Bank
ASEAN	Association of Southeast Asian Nations
B-I-G Program	Brunei Darussalam–Indonesia–Malaysia–Philippines East ASEAN Growth Area (BIMP-EAGA), the Indonesia–Malaysia–Thailand Growth Triangle (IMT-GT), and the Greater Mekong Subregion (GMS) Capacity Building Program
BIMP-EAGA	Brunei Darussalam–Indonesia–Malaysia–Philippines East ASEAN Growth Area
COVAX	COVID-19 Vaccines Global Access
COVID-19	coronavirus disease
CPTA	Cross-Border Paperless Trade in Asia and the Pacific
DMC	developing member country
ESCAP	Economic and Social Commission for Asia and the Pacific
ETM	Energy Transition Mechanism
GMS	Greater Mekong Subregion
GHG	greenhouse gas
GW	gigawatt
IMT-GT	Indonesia–Malaysia–Thailand Growth Triangle
IMDA	Infocomm Media Development Authority
IRENA	International Renewable Energy Agency
ISO	International Organization for Standardization
IT	information technology
LEI	Legal Entity Identifier
MLETR	Model Law on Electronic Transferable Records
MSMEs	micro, small, and medium-sized enterprises
NDC	nationally determined contribution
PACER	Policy Actions for COVID-19 Economic Recovery
SDG	Sustainable Development Goal
TESDA	Technical Education and Skills Development Authority
TVET	technical and vocational education and training
UNCITRAL	United Nations Commission on International Trade Law
US	United States
VECOM	Viet Nam E-Commerce Association
WHO	World Health Organization

Executive Summary

Ramesh Subramaniam
Director General and Chief, Sectors Group, Asia and the Pacific, ADB

Alfredo Perdiguero
Regional Head, Regional Cooperation and Integration, SERD, ADB

Jason Rush
Principal Regional Cooperation Specialist, SERD, ADB

Pamela Asis-Layugan
Institutional and Capacity Development Specialist (International Consultant), SERD, ADB

Chapter 1: Fostering Resilient Recovery

The coronavirus disease (COVID-19) pandemic triggered a multidimensional crisis like no other across Southeast Asia and other parts of the world. The magnitude of the crisis severely affected lives and livelihoods. A resilient health system and a future-ready workforce are crucial to resilient recovery.

The immense responsibility of delivering billions of vaccine doses calls for strategic partnerships and collaboration with the international community. **Jerome Kim** underscores the need for whole-of-government and whole-of-society approaches in addressing the various components and complexities of vaccine distribution and engaging multiple actors. In Asia, regional cooperation can be instrumental in facilitating data sharing and harmonizing regulatory policies, which can help reduce time lags in vaccine delivery.

Dealing with COVID-19 goes beyond the immediate crisis and requires instituting reforms to build the resilience of technical and vocational education and training (TVET) systems and identify concrete measures for the recovery and rejuvenation phases. **Sameer Khatiwada** and **Rosanna Urdaneta** offer policy measures that can build a competitive workforce and shape labor market outcomes amid the twin challenges of managing the impact of COVID-19 and thriving in the Fourth Industrial Revolution (4IR).

Chapter 2: Promoting Trade Digitization

Despite significant challenges to economic growth, the COVID-19 crisis has brought about a dramatic uptake of digital technologies across Southeast Asian countries. In 2020, a report on the internet economy prepared by Google, Singapore's Temasek, and Bain and Company in Southeast Asia's six largest economies—Indonesia, Malaysia, Singapore, Thailand, the Philippines, and Viet Nam—noted that 40 million people went online in these countries for the first time in 2020, thus raising the total number of internet users in the Association of

Southeast Asian Nations (ASEAN) to 400 million, up by 62.5% compared with 250 million users in 2015. This figure comprises about 70% of the 580 million total population in these six ASEAN member states. The size of ASEAN's internet economy in 2020 exceeded $100 billion for the first time. Assuming the trends will be sustained, it can increase threefold to $300 billion by 2025. In addition, the report found that 94% of new digital service customers intend to keep the service even after the pandemic.

Oswald Kuyler, Luca Castellani, Sin Yong Loh, and **Kobsak Duangdee** discuss how digitization of trade leads to greater efficiencies to support economies in the post-pandemic world and improve the resilience of the global economic system. They emphasized that digitalization's array of benefits—from traceability to real-time tracking, faster clearance of shipments, prevention of fraud, and reduced compliance costs—can only be realized if a robust domestic legal environment for electronic transferable records is in place alongside industry-wide collaboration, capacity building, and sharing success stories to improve buy-in, among others.

Regional cooperation can support a well-functioning enabling environment and fast-track the growth of the digital economy. **Satvinder Singh** and **Mario Masa** outline how an enabling environment in ASEAN can fast-track the growth of the digital economy. ASEAN has accelerated e-commerce through intergovernmental mechanisms and frameworks. Policy actions on pivotal issues across the different segments of the e-commerce value chain (government, private sector, and broader community) are proposed, including institutional measures; trust and recognition; talent, innovation, and capacity building; and seamless connectivity.

Viet Nam's economy has shown resilience relative to its ASEAN neighbors amid the COVID-19 crisis and recognizes e-commerce as pivotal in economic recovery. **Le The Phuc** shares Viet Nam's experience in harnessing e-commerce and prioritizing policy actions rooted in its key enablers of connectivity, digital payments, skills development, logistics systems, cybersecurity, and consumer trust.

Chapter 3: Accelerating Green Recovery, Clean Energy, and Circular Economy Transitions

The final chapter examines how countries can reorient their economies toward a more sustainable trajectory. Low-carbon policies and green national recovery strategies must mitigate the risks of future pandemics, address climate change, and improve competitiveness. Green policies and strategies will also guide investors, businesses, workers, and consumers toward sustainability, which can be determined by frameworks for sustainable finance and taxonomy principles. The chapter also highlights regional cooperation responses in clean energy transition, green recovery, and transition to circular systems.

As Southeast Asian countries repair their battered economies wrought by the pandemic, policy makers are afforded the unique opportunity to determine the type of economic recovery they will pursue. Will they choose measures that reinforce existing economic structures, particularly those negatively impacting the environment? Or will they see the COVID-19 crisis as an opportunity to rebuild in a way that significantly transforms environmental outcomes?

Anouj Mehta highlights green growth opportunities and what is needed to scale up green finance to support governments' recovery plans. A three-step approach toward implementing green recovery in Southeast Asia includes (i) building mechanisms that can produce a lasting shift toward ecosystem resilience; (ii) implementing targeted policy interventions focused on five areas of opportunity in regenerative agriculture, sustainable urban development and transport models, clean energy transition, circular economy models, and healthy and productive oceans; and (iii) identifying sustainable sources of financing.

Pradeep Tharakan promotes policy prescriptions to foster clean energy transition, support energy efficiency at scale, expand access to green finance, enhance regional power trade, encourage accelerated retirement and repurposing of fossil fuel-based power generation assets, apply clean energy deployment as an economic recovery tool, and raise the ambition of climate policies and develop global cooperation.

Shifting from a "take, make, waste" to a circular system can spur green growth and contribute to post-pandemic revival strategies. The circular economy helps build more resilient economies, create new jobs, harness innovations and technologies, establish green supply chains, and extend product life cycles.

James Baker showcases that a systems approach with integrated and holistic policies from both the supply and demand sides is vital to push an ambitious agenda that requires capital and innovation coupled with transformative models and mindsets. With Southeast Asia's strong economic integration agenda, it is imperative to foster coherence in formulating and coordinating circular economic policies at the regional level to address fragmentation.

Vandana Dhaul argues that shifting to circular approaches can deliver economic gains and, more importantly, address food security and promote sustainable production and consumption. Options for reducing waste both upstream and downstream in the agrifood value chain include tradable credits to reduce food waste, innovative financing instruments that support projects, insect farming for feed and food production, collaboration between companies and farmers, campaigns and policies to curb consumer waste behavior, and research and development to promote valorization opportunities.

CHAPTER 1
Fostering Resilient Recovery

Managing Safe, Equitable, and Effective COVID-19 Vaccination

Jerome Kim
Director General, International Vaccine Institute

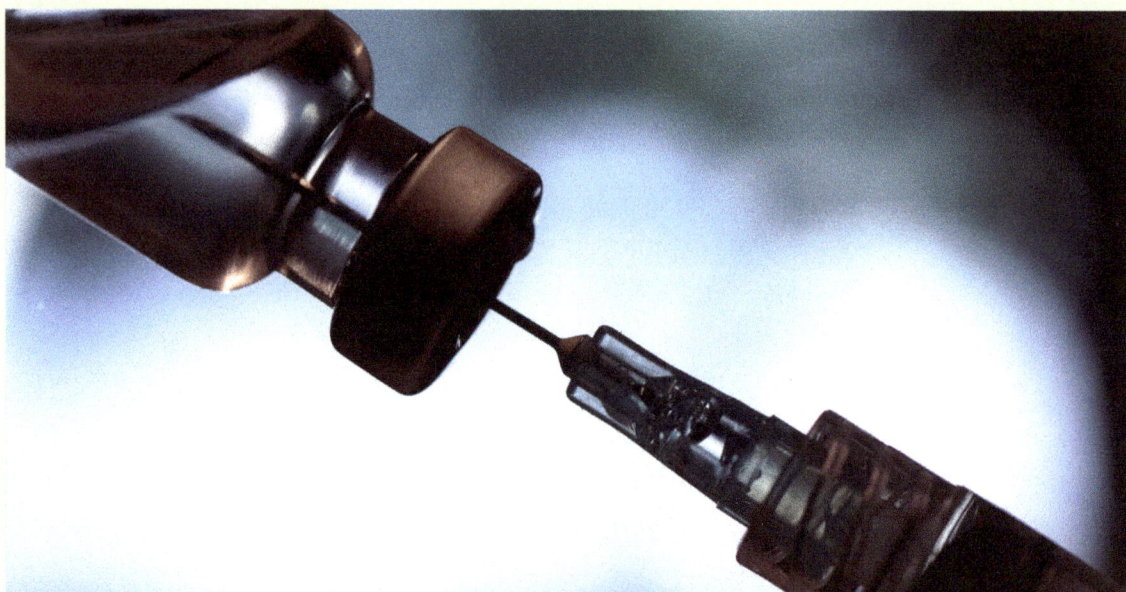

COVID-19 vaccination. Regional cooperation can facilitate data sharing and harmonization of regulatory policies among countries to ensure the timely delivery of vaccines (photo by ADB).

Introduction

The concerted global endeavor to curb the spread of the coronavirus disease (COVID-19) has brought not just one but multiple novel vaccines with signals of efficacy and safety in less than a year since the declaration of COVID-19 as a pandemic. This is an astonishing scientific achievement. In 2021, 10 vaccines underwent regulatory reviews in their respective countries.[1] Four vaccines—Pfizer/BioNTech, Oxford/AstraZeneca, Moderna, and Johnson & Johnson—were approved by the World Health Organization (WHO) for emergency use.

Yet, a vaccine is only a weapon in the fight against the pandemic. Immunizing billions of people requires a comprehensive strategy of prevention, logistical infrastructure, an army of vaccinators, safety monitoring and evaluation systems, and a receptive public. International cooperation is also vital to ensure fair access to vaccines, achieve global herd immunity, and end the pandemic.

---

[1]   Pfizer, Moderna, Astra Zeneca, Johnson & Johnson, Gamaleya, Sinopharm (2), Sinovac, Novavax, Bharat, and CanSino.

With the arrival of vaccines, country efforts to address the impacts of the crisis are now centered on mass vaccination campaigns. High-income countries are already vaccinating their populations and have generally secured sufficient supply. Low- and middle-income countries are in various stages of negotiations and procurement, and some commenced inoculations in early 2021. In Southeast Asia, mass vaccinations in most nations are not anticipated to be fully implemented until 2022. As most of the low-resource economies in the region get left behind due to the global competition over limited doses, they face the threat of dangerous new strains of the virus.

Data modeling suggests that developed countries would likewise suffer enormous human and economic costs if vaccine nationalism persists, defeating their purpose of protecting their populations. The global economic cost associated with the pandemic is approximately $4 trillion–$5 trillion, 49% of which is borne by the advanced economies despite universal vaccination in their countries.

Challenges in Vaccination

The vaccine itself does not save lives; vaccination does. To conduct large-scale immunization programs, governments must address a myriad of challenges including supply constraints, investments in logistics and cold chain equipment, training of health personnel, and public hesitation about vaccines.

Although many viable COVID-19 vaccines show efficacy and safety results, the shortage of doses is obstructing several countries' path out of the pandemic, especially for low-resource economies. The COVID-19 Vaccines Global Access (COVAX) Facility is supporting the procurement of vaccines at low or no cost to provide equitable and reliable access to low- and middle-income countries, as high-income countries have largely secured sufficient vaccines to protect their citizenry. However, it covers only the vaccines with WHO approval and signed contracts with the facility.[2] In December 2022, COVAX delivered 2 billion doses to 146 countries and helped 40 countries start their vaccination campaigns.

Scaling up production capacity that adheres to high quality standards is no easy feat. The number of doses is also contingent on the availability of manufacturing materials and ancillary vaccine supplies. Pfizer/BioNTech, for instance, encountered production delays when early batches of raw materials failed to meet quality standards.

It is anticipated that some products in the vaccine pipeline will eventually get approved for emergency use, thereby helping boost the supply of doses. Still, countries need contingency plans as the possibility of quality control, and supply chain problems may arise.

Equally important to the availability of supply is the distribution logistics, as different types of COVID-19 vaccines have different handling and storage requirements.[3] Adding to the complexities of logistics is limited air transport capacity due to disruptions to flights and airport operations during the pandemic. According to

---

[2]   Pfizer/BioNTech, Oxford/AstraZeneca, and Johnson & Johnson COVID-19 vaccines are part of COVAX and approved by WHO for emergency use.

[3]   Pfizer/BioNTech and Moderna COVID-19 vaccines require −25°C to −15°C and −20°C, respectively, for storage temperature. Oxford/AstraZeneca, Gamaleya Sinopharm, Sinovac, Novavax, Johnson & Johnson, and CanSino vaccines need to be kept at 2–8°C.

the International Air Transport Association, 8,000 jumbo cargo jets would be needed to deliver a single dose to each of the world's 7.8 billion people.

Beyond cold chain and transport infrastructure, safe storage and handling of vaccines depend on the knowledge and practices of health personnel. Countries need to allocate resources for the training of technicians and medical staff on prevailing guidelines, administering of different types of vaccines, the systematic monitoring of any adverse events, and the efficacy of vaccines administered against emerging virus mutations. Health systems also face the challenge of adjusting existing delivery strategies that have largely been focused on child immunization as they shift to adult vaccinations and significantly expand coverage.

Finally, vaccine hesitancy poses a major threat to the collective goal of getting the COVID-19 pandemic under control. Safety concerns should be alleviated by explaining the science behind the COVID-19 vaccines and addressing the factors that drive mistrust around vaccines, including an enabling environment, social influences, and motivation.

Policy Options

Multi-stakeholder planning with prioritization of doses

Strategic planning involving multiple stakeholders across sectors is fundamental to the success of vaccine delivery efforts. This process entails planning for scenarios, developing a national vaccine strategy, and organizing the operational aspects of vaccine introduction.

Due to the lack of doses, strategy development requires prioritization of target groups and distribution of vaccines in a phased manner. Although the priority allocation models of different countries may vary based on their local conditions, the common framework focuses on health workers and segments with health vulnerabilities as priority recipients. Countries may also prioritize essential workers aside from those in the health sector to jump-start their economies.

Investments in infrastructure and human resources

Along with financing for acquiring vaccines, countries need to allocate investments in distribution and delivery systems such as cold chain equipment. Fortunately, most vaccines with emergency use authorization only need conventional cold chain, but investments are still necessary for ramping up distribution, especially in remote areas.

Efforts should also include strengthening the capacity of personnel and enforcing proper cold chain management practices. It is important to have a system for tracking the safety of vaccines administered and identifying the vaccine product associated with an adverse event as well as its batch or lot number.

Connectivity, border management, and security

With the restricted movement of people and goods during the pandemic, governments need measures to prioritize the entry of approved vaccines in their country. Border processes should include expedited clearance procedures for COVID-19 vaccines and tariff relief to facilitate their shipment.

Since customs requirements and varying trade regulations can hamper the timely distribution of vaccines, there should be streamlined and transparent border processes. At the same time, appropriate security protocols must be in place to thwart deviation and counterfeiting. Because COVID-19 vaccines are highly in-demand commodities, deploying security solutions that prevent tampering or theft throughout the supply chain is imperative.

Partnerships and regional cooperation

The immense undertaking of delivering billions of doses calls for strategic partnerships and collaboration with the international community. In Asia, regional cooperation can be instrumental in facilitating data sharing and harmonizing regulatory policies, which can aid in reducing time lags in vaccine delivery. Since the region is home to vaccine manufacturing hubs, governments should form partnerships to accelerate the production of doses and consider donating their excess supply to other countries still experiencing uncontrolled outbreaks.

The private sector is also critical in scaling up and strengthening medical supply chains to preserve the integrity of vaccines and deliver them on time. Capitalizing on the networks of shipping, airline, and logistics companies, alongside their strong infrastructure and information technology (IT)-enabled supply chains, will allow governments to optimize distribution and ensure transparency of every shipment.

Transparency and communications

Advocacy and communications should be incorporated into the strategic plans of governments for vaccine deployment and delivery. Governments may consider partnering with influential people who can advocate for COVID-19 vaccination drives and support the efforts of governments to reach target groups.

There should be timely and frequent communications, and governments should openly and transparently communicate with the public when adverse events occur. Similarly, governments should be upfront about the unknowns at this stage. Since the immunity duration from COVID-19 vaccines is still unclear, governments should inform the public that the length of protection from vaccination still requires further study.

Policy Implementation and Outcomes

According to Our World in Data, more than 1 billion doses of COVID-19 vaccines have been administered globally. Distributions in rich countries are outpacing those in lower-income economies.

To date, Israel and Seychelles are the fastest to roll out inoculations, with about 60% of their populations fully vaccinated. While the rapid deployment of vaccines has been facilitated by Israel's adequate resources and quality health-care systems, its wealth of data has served as a valuable currency to secure doses from Pfizer/BioNTech. With the country's digitized health systems, the government has agreed to exchange extensive data on its inoculation program with Pfizer/BioNTech, which is crucial to generate insights into the long-term safety and efficacy of the vaccine.

In the United States (US), the rollout initially encountered some hurdles but is now accelerating. Pharmacies have played a critical role in delivering COVID-19 shots by making it easier for people to get vaccinated. In addition to proximity, pharmacies are optimal for the mass vaccination drive because Americans are already accustomed to getting their flu shots in such locations.

In Asia, countries leading in the vaccination drive are Maldives with 73.92 doses administered for every 100 people; Bhutan, 62.27 doses; Mongolia, 46.75 doses; and Singapore, 37.84 doses. The People's Republic of China is also one of the countries rapidly accelerating its inoculation efforts, with 19.45 doses administered for every 100 people. This is followed by Azerbaijan (14.96), Cambodia (14.77), India (11.31), Kazakhstan (8.31), and Indonesia (7.38). These positive developments, particularly in South Asian countries, could be attributed to their manufacturing capabilities and regional cooperation.

In Bhutan, its vaccination campaign was only launched at the end of March, yet more than 90% of its adult population had already been given the first shot of Oxford/AstraZeneca vaccines donated by India. Granted that the country's small population gives it an advantage over other nations, dedicated volunteers and a robust health-care system are the key factors propelling rapid vaccine rollout.

In Asia and the Pacific, the Asian Development Bank (ADB) launched the Asia Pacific Vaccine Access Facility to support the efforts of developing member countries (DMCs) to procure safe and effective vaccines. This $9 billion initiative includes a rapid response component that provides timely support for critical vaccine diagnostics, procurement, and transport from the place of purchase to DMCs and a project investment component to support investments in systems for the delivery and administration of vaccines along with associated investments in capacity building, community outreach, and surveillance. The program may also help develop or expand vaccine manufacturing capacity in the DMCs.

In Indonesia, for example, its state-owned vaccine supplier, Bio Farma, will be provided financing through the Asia Pacific Vaccine Access Facility for vaccine procurement. ADB's $450 million assistance will also help the government and Bio Farma improve logistics management and deliver vaccines more effectively.

Public–private partnerships are also proving valuable in distributing COVID-19 vaccines at scale. The United Nations Children's Fund (UNICEF) and the World Economic Forum signed a charter with shipping, airlines, and logistics companies such as DHL and Maersk to support the distribution of COVID-19 vaccines, with prioritization and solutions for the international and in-country distribution of vaccines and related supplies on behalf of COVAX.

Singapore partnered with DHL to ship its first batch of vaccines from Belgium. Technologies, such as temperature trackers equipped with GPS, are placed in thermal shipper boxes to enable full visibility throughout the shipment's entire journey.

The Government of Ghana has forged partnerships with UPS Foundation and Zipline, a medical drone delivery company. Up to 2.5 million doses will be delivered via drones to vaccination sites to not only improve the speed of distribution but also expand the scope of vaccination efforts, increasing access to hard-to-reach areas.

In the Philippines and other parts of Asia, Zuellig Pharma has expanded its cold storage warehouse capacity in response to the storage and distribution demands of COVID-19 vaccines. Its cold chain management uses eZTracker, a blockchain solution enabling full traceability during vaccine distribution to ensure integrity.

Within the health care sector, notable alliances are driving the expansion of manufacturing capacities across various countries. The Serum Institute of India's partnership with AstraZeneca helps scale up the production of Oxford/AstraZeneca vaccine doses, which many low-income countries depend on. Bio Farma has teamed up with Sinovac to provide the technology licensing of CoronaVac for production in Indonesia. Merck is working with Johnson & Johnson to help boost the supply of its single-shot COVID-19 vaccine, which got emergency authorization from the US Food and Drug Administration and WHO.

To boost public trust in COVID-19 vaccines, politicians and influential figures have used their platforms to share their own experiences in getting vaccinated. For instance, the heads of the governments of the US, Israel, Indonesia, and India received shots publicly to create a degree of confidence for the public. Similarly, celebrities are playing their part in spreading awareness of the importance of vaccination.

Recommendations

An unprecedented challenge calls for whole-of-government and whole-of-society approaches

The various components and complexities of vaccine distribution—including determining priority groups, dealing with the variance in storage and logistical requirements of different vaccines, engaging with communities, and collecting information—require the participation of multiple actors to carry out a task of this magnitude. Multisector approaches can enable policy coherence to facilitate the timely, effective, and efficient distribution and administration of vaccines.

Collecting data is crucial to vaccine prioritization and post-market surveillance

COVID-19 has magnified the value of data in policymaking. Prioritizing the allocation of vaccines demands investments in effective and efficient data collection to provide a better understanding of which groups have underlying health conditions. Data are likewise integral to monitoring outcomes after the COVID-19 vaccination and investigating any adverse effects in relation to different types of vaccines.

Influential figures could be strong assets in public health campaigns

A large-scale vaccination drive may require innovative approaches to public health communications. Campaigns could be more effective by involving celebrities or influencers that resonate with communities exhibiting low confidence in COVID-19 vaccines. These vaccine campaigns should be engaging and comprehensible, and anchored in science. Public health communication strategies should be customized to connect with people of different age groups that reach them through the right channels.

Continue to uphold standards for COVID-19 infection prevention even after vaccination

Because it is still unclear whether the available vaccines can prevent COVID-19 transmission, reminding the public about maintaining infection control measures such as wearing masks and social distancing is essential. Data suggest that the vaccines can protect people from developing serious symptoms of the disease, but transmissions could still occur. It is also important to note that only a portion of the population will be vaccinated in the early stages of the rollout. Thus, governments must urge the public to still follow prevention protocols.

Resources

Centers for Disease Control and Prevention. The Federal Retail Pharmacy Program for COVID-19 Vaccination.

International Air Transport Association (IATA). 2020. Guidance for Vaccine and Pharmaceutical Logistics and Distribution. 16 December.

Kim, Kim. 2021. COVID-19 Vaccines Update. Presented at the Policy Actions for COVID-19 Economic Recovery Dialogues of the Asian Development Bank. Webinar. 24 February.

O'Donnell, C. 2020. Pfizer Says Supply Chain Challenges Contributed to Slashed Target for COVID-19 Vaccine Doses in 2020. *Reuters*. 4 December.

Park, C. et al. 2021. Getting Ready for the COVID-19 Vaccine Rollout. *ADB Briefs*. No. 166.

The Future of Skills Development in the Time of COVID-19

Sameer Khatiwada
Senior Public Management Economist, Sectors Group, Asian Development Bank

Rosanna Urdaneta
Deputy Director General, Technical Education and Skills Development Authority (TESDA), Philippines

Automation of routine jobs. National skills strategies should consider the growing trend toward automation of routine jobs for efficiency and profitability (photo by ADB).

Introduction

The Fourth Industrial Revolution (4IR) is reshaping the world of work, altering business models, and requiring a new set of skills for workers to thrive in an increasingly competitive environment. Disruptions to the labor market are compounded by the impact of the coronavirus disease (COVID-19), widening inequities and accentuating the importance of investments in reskilling and upskilling to help displaced workers get new jobs. The twin shocks are catapulting economies into a more technology-driven world, thereby cementing the value of digital skills.

As Asian countries look toward their post-pandemic recovery, policy makers need to use the digital momentum to rethink education and employment, including technical and vocational education and training (TVET) systems, to become better positioned for 4IR. Skills development and work readiness are the hallmarks of TVET and have a crucial role in shaping labor market outcomes and responding and adapting to 4IR. Dealing with

COVID-19 goes beyond the immediate crisis and requires instituting reforms to build the resilience of TVET systems and identify concrete measures for the recovery and rejuvenation phases.

Challenges and Opportunities

Changing labor market conditions driven by the speed of technological progress have painted a worrying picture of the employment landscape. Concerns over robots replacing workers, technologies rendering some industries obsolete, and other potential perils of 4IR abound.

However, an ADB study largely offers an encouraging outlook for Southeast Asia. The positive income effects of 4IR adoption in the key industries examined across Cambodia, Indonesia, the Philippines, and Viet Nam will outweigh the negative displacement effects. By 2030, job creation will be greater than displacement in all analyzed industries.

To realize the net gains from 4IR, countries need to prepare for automation, which will be particularly pronounced in low-skilled and routine jobs. Even though opportunities may surface from the wave of innovations, displaced workers may encounter challenges in transitioning to new jobs. The rate of digital transformation may outpace efforts to retool and upskill talent, potentially leading to a supply and demand mismatch. ADB's analysis notes that productivity gains from 4IR, which are expected to increase income and create jobs, may take years to materialize.

Measures to prevent the spread of COVID-19, such as movement restrictions and lockdowns, laid bare the preexisting inequities in the labor market. Many low-skilled workers and rural inhabitants are in occupations with low teleworkability, making them highly vulnerable. Informal workers, who depend on their daily wages to survive with minimal social protection, risk plunging into extreme poverty. Gender gaps are starkly apparent as women bear the brunt of the crisis due to increased domestic responsibilities. Gender inequity may perpetuate or even worsen under 4IR given the predominance of women in precarious work.

Education and training institutions were also ill-prepared to cope with the COVID-19 challenges of providing online learning, possibly due to weak information technology (IT) infrastructure, IT skills gap of learners and teachers, and limited access to digital resources.

Building a 4IR-ready workforce necessitates anticipating the shifts in skill requirements prompted by emerging technologies. ADB's findings show that training institutions are more optimistic about the graduates' preparedness for work than employers. For example, 96% of training institutions in Indonesia believe that their graduates are well prepared for work, but only 33% of employers in food and beverage manufacturing and 30% of employers in automotive manufacturing agree. If left unaddressed, this gap is likely to widen as digitalization unfolds. Other issues uncovered by the study include limited incentives for formal workplace training, weak lifelong learning models, and lack of agility of educational curricula.

Policy Options

Develop 4IR transformation road maps for key sectors

To maximize 4IR's productivity benefits and minimize job displacement, policy makers need to develop an implementation strategy that drives 4IR technological adoption while ensuring workers acquire and upgrade skills. Industry-specific transformation maps may provide information on technology impacts, skills required for different occupations, career pathways, and the appropriate reskilling interventions.

Develop industry-led TVET programs targeting skills for 4IR

TVET programs would greatly benefit from the involvement of industry associations, which can help ensure the quality and relevance of the courses being offered. It is paramount for educational institutions to constantly rethink and update their curricula to align programs with the needs of the 4IR economy, which will likely place a premium on critical thinking, technological proficiency, and soft skills including creativity and problem-solving. These in-demand skills may also be cultivated through workplace-based trainings, facilitating better coherence between education and work and easing the transition for students when they enter the workforce.

Upgrade training delivery through 4IR technology in classrooms and training facilities

At the core of 4IR is technology-driven change. Thus, it is critical to support investments in smart technologies for TVET delivery, such as virtual and augmented reality as well as digital capacity building for TVET instructors. A hybrid approach to 4IR instruction can be an optimal solution to not only help TVET institutions manage the costs of procuring tools and equipment but also accommodate learners at a digital disadvantage.

Develop flexible and modular skills certification programs

There is scope for expanding learning opportunities beyond school boundaries to foster workers' resilience against current and future shocks. Navigating a world of disruptions requires a culture of lifelong learning to help workers become agile, adaptable, and responsive to a dynamic economy. Equally crucial is the development of a flexible skills qualification program given the rising demand for modular learning and the need for recognition of skills acquired through nontraditional channels.

Formulate new approaches and measures to strengthen inclusion and social protection under 4IR

Responding to the evolving nature of work necessitates rethinking the social contract. As demonstrated by COVID-19, there is a strong need for social safety net provisions to protect workers from shocks, regardless of their employment status. Informality is a persistent issue in Asia, and freelance jobs are anticipated to proliferate owing to a booming gig economy. Therefore, social protection becomes even more vital.

In promoting inclusion, policy makers should pursue measures to ensure vulnerable segments of the population have access to skills training for 4IR. One way to do this is to use educational technologies, such as massive open online courses, which provide learning opportunities at a low cost.

Implement an incentive scheme for firms to train employees for 4IR

The onus of skills development not only lies with the education sector but also with the business sector. Incentive programs can encourage investments in skills development. These programs need to be supplemented with measures to increase awareness of businesses on upskilling and reskilling opportunities.

To gauge the effectiveness of incentive schemes and training interventions on labor outcomes, the government should conduct a holistic cost–benefit analysis, considering the direct economic costs and indirect economic benefits.

Policy Implementation

Over the years, the Technical Education and Skills Development Authority (TESDA) in the Philippines has embarked on notable reforms, including the institutionalization of the Philippine Qualifications Framework, which reinforces and strengthens the recognition of knowledge and skills acquired outside the formal education environment through a system of pathways, equivalencies, and credit transfers. Another significant development in the Philippine education sector is the K-12 reform, extending formal education to align with international norms and incorporating a distinct technical–vocational and livelihood track into the senior high school program.

Guided by its two-pronged strategy of TVET for Global Competitiveness and TVET for Social Equity, TESDA seeks to equip Filipino workers with 4IR skills and offer quality training. Using inclusive approaches, such as community-based training and scholarships, it endeavors to expand TVET access and respond to local needs.

TVETPH 4.0 Framework was developed to maximize opportunities brought by 4IR and ensure the right competencies are imparted to learners, trainers, and institutions. With the onset of the pandemic, OPLAN TESDA Abot Lahat: TVET towards the New Normal was developed as a continuity plan to shift TESDA's systems, processes, and programs into the new normal. Flexible learning arrangements were introduced for TVET schools to utilize different delivery modes: distance learning, face-to-face learning, online learning, and blended learning. The TESDA Online program provided accessible and continued learning to Filipinos during the lockdowns.

In Singapore, the SkillsFuture movement is a national skills strategy to help build the foundation for a highly skilled, productive, and innovative economy. The program facilitates industry exposure through work–study programs for students and learning opportunities for workers at different points in their careers. The private sector and industry stakeholders play a role in shaping the development of SkillsFuture initiatives by participating in the development of industry transformation maps and skills frameworks and providing employee training. For education and training institutions, the program aids the transformation of course delivery to ensure the flexibility and accessibility of learning.

Similarly, other Southeast Asian countries have established a range of policies in relation to 4IR. Cambodia and Indonesia have clear national 4IR road maps, with Indonesia having assessed 4IR readiness in five priority sectors to guide specific 4IR technology adoption strategies for firms in each sector. In Viet Nam, lifelong learning appears to be a strong focus area driven by its network of local learning centers where training courses are offered. When it comes to collaboration, Cambodia, Indonesia, and Viet Nam underscore partnerships with employers, educators, and training institutions on skills development and offer demonstration of new technologies to stimulate company adoption and facilitate worker training through innovation hubs.

Policy Outcomes

While the ADB study explored the implications of 4IR in selected Southeast Asian countries, the following outcomes focus on the Philippines. ADB conducted a comprehensive review of the country's TVET sector in the 4IR context, along with the changing demand for labor in light of COVID-19.

The study finds that TVET in the Philippines is estimated to be an economically viable alternative to tertiary education, which entails higher direct and indirect costs. Despite representing less than 10% of TVET providers, public institutions accounted for 52% of the country's TVET enrollment in 2018. While returns to TVET differ depending on the level and the course, the post-secondary and tertiary levels exhibit largely positive returns.

Figure 1.1: Returns to Post-Secondary Non-Tertiary Education
(Lower Secondary Graduates as Reference)

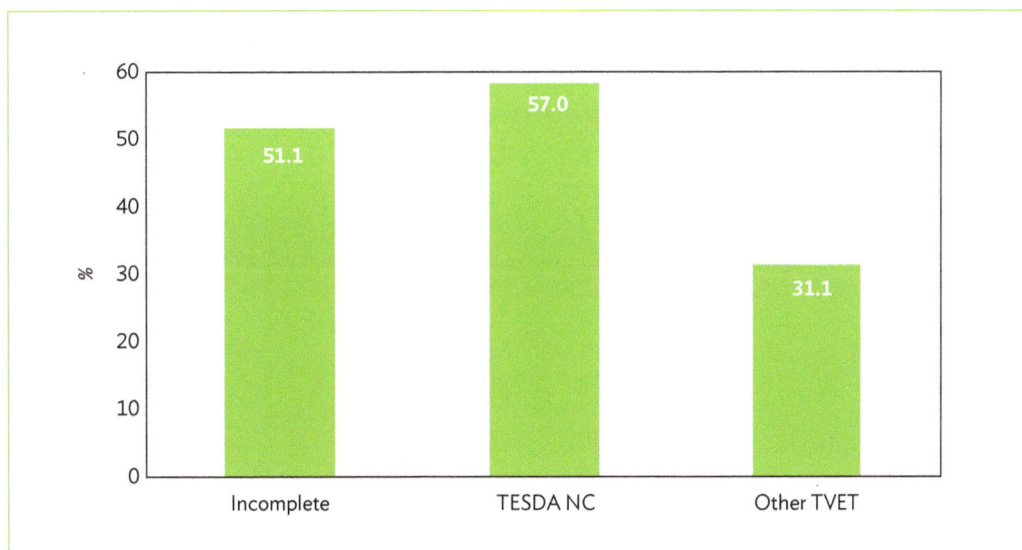

TESDA NC = Technical Education and Skills Development Authority National Certification, TVET = technical and vocational education and training.
[a]<0.05
[b]<0.01
[c]<0.001
Source: Asian Development Bank estimates.

Another key point from ADB's assessment highlights the detrimental impact of the education and skills mismatch on TVET graduates' employability. This problem is attributed to the inability to keep the training curriculum, course offerings, and training equipment relevant to the job market. Using simple matching, TVET graduates recorded high mismatch rates ranging from 42% to 82% in 2013, 2014, and 2017.

Figure 1.2: Mismatch Rates Using Simple Matching Technique, 2013, 2014, and 2017 Graduates

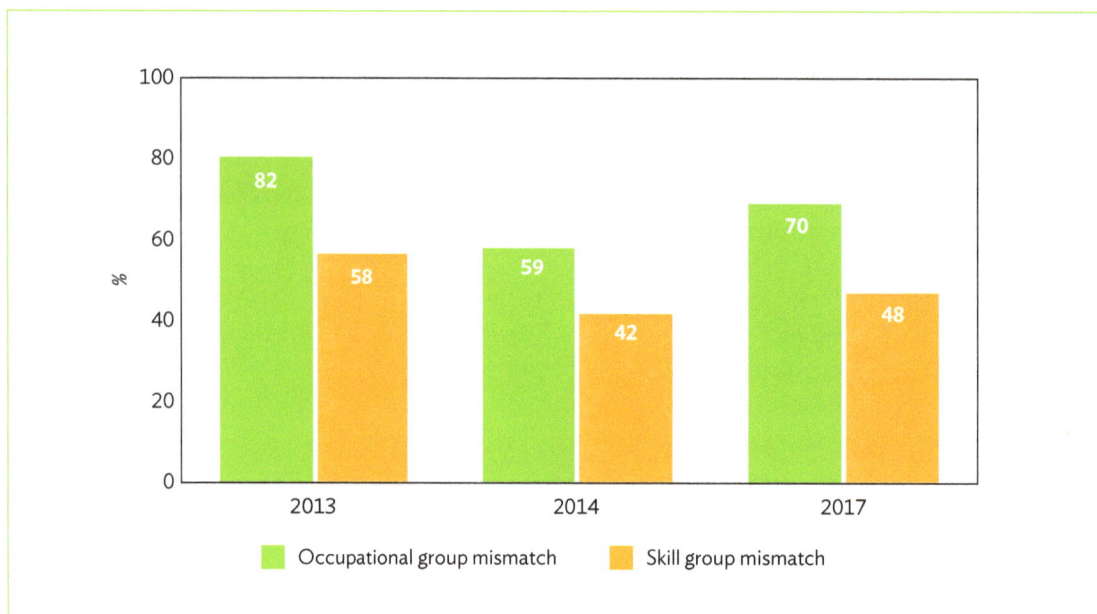

Source: Asian Development Bank estimates.

Findings also suggest that while the scholarships largely satisfy the objective of social equity, much improvement is needed in promoting competitiveness and productivity. Finally, although top courses in terms of TVET enrollment in recent years reflect growth sectors of the Philippine economy, these programs often lead to low-wage, low-productivity, and nonroutine manual jobs, which are susceptible to automation.

Recommendations

Stimulate 4IR adoption and worker reskilling efforts

In a post-pandemic environment, building agile and responsive TVET systems calls for the adoption of 4IR across enterprises and the workforce, greater participation of firms and workers in skills development, and strong awareness of in-demand jobs and skills. A whole-of-government-and-society approach is crucial to facilitating an aligned ecosystem to create relevant and effective nationwide retraining frameworks and catalyze quality jobs.

As micro, small, and medium-sized enterprises (MSMEs) may face hurdles in adopting 4IR technologies, there is a need to deepen efforts to support 4IR knowledge transfer from large companies to their MSME suppliers or subcontractors.

Create flexible qualification pathways

Lifelong learning is the antidote to shifting patterns of skills demand. As nonlinear careers are the new normal, workers must be able to navigate through multiple job transitions. Policy makers need to focus on improving the skills and competitiveness of workers to support economic diversification and reduce reliance on only a few economic sectors or external demand. Policies should also be geared toward making curricula more reflective of industry needs and developing a flexible qualification framework for employment.

Build inclusiveness to extend 4IR benefits to workers

With the profound implications of 4IR—especially on women, informal workers, and marginalized groups, the imperative to strengthen social protection has never been clearer. Labor market programs can play a greater role in social protection systems to diminish vulnerable workers' risk exposure.

In addition, technology should be harnessed to improve access to quality TVET and opportunities for all. Online platforms and advanced technology solutions could support 4IR instruction, but it is also important to keep in mind equity considerations in terms of access, affordability, and infrastructure. Finally, if young people are to benefit from 4IR, policies should seek to bridge the aspiration gap through mechanisms that can guide them to envision their prospects and tools that allow them to achieve career goals.

Resources

Asian Development Bank (ADB). 2021. *Reaping the Benefits of Industry 4.0 through Skills Development in High-Growth Industries in Southeast Asia: Insights from Cambodia, Indonesia, the Philippines, and Viet Nam*. Manila.

_____. 2021. *Technical and Vocational Education and Training in the Philippines in the Age of Industry 4.0*. Manila.

Khatiwada, S. 2021. Future of Skills Development in the Time of COVID-19. Presented at the Policy Actions for COVID-19 Economic Recovery Dialogues of the Asian Development Bank. 10 June.

Urdaneta, R. 2021. Transforming TVET in the Philippines: Dealing with COVID-19 in the Age of Industry 4.0. Presented at the Policy Actions for COVID-19 Economic Recovery Dialogues of the Asian Development Bank. 10 June.

CHAPTER 2
Promoting Trade Digitization

Enabling the Digital Transformation of Global Trade in the New Normal

Farzana Muhib
Digital Standards Initiative Managing Director, International Chamber of Commerce (ICC)

Luca Castellani
Legal Officer, United Nations Commission on International Trade Law (UNCITRAL)

Sin Yong Loh
Director for Trade, Infocomm Media Development Authority of Singapore (IMDA)

Kobsak Duangdee
Secretary General, Thai Bankers' Association (TBA), Thailand

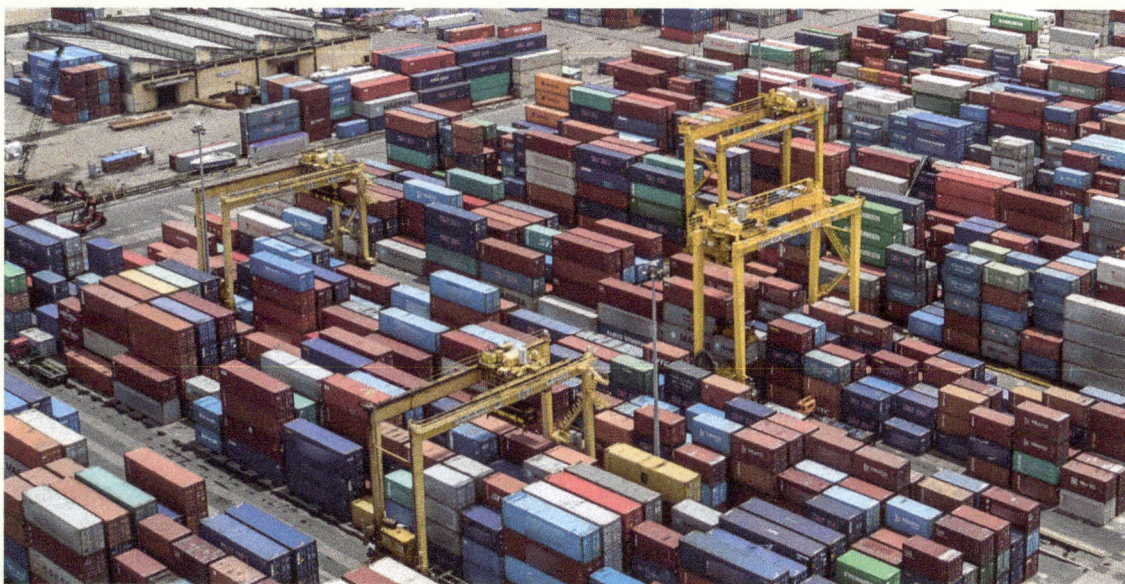

Cargoes. Largely paper-driven, the global trade system is plagued with multiple requirements, complex documentation flows, and information asymmetry (photo by ADB).

Introduction

With the widespread shift to online channels among businesses and consumers during the coronavirus disease (COVID-19) outbreak, e-commerce surged in Asia and the rest of the world. In 2021, Alibaba Group's shopping app Lazada onboarded 70,000 merchants to its platform.

Before the pandemic, there was already an upward trend in the digital market in Asia. Yet, the uptake of cross-border paperless trade has been dismal.

The pandemic hampered supply chains and exposed the shortcomings of paper-based processes, which were slowed down by lockdowns imposed by countries. The Suez Canal blockage was another exogenous shock that clogged a vital artery in global trade and underscored the inefficiencies of its manual systems. But amid the disruptions, these events have also served as a catalyst for scaling up the digitalization of supply chains and fostering resilience in the global trading system, which are crucial for rebuilding economies beyond the pandemic.

Paper-Intensive Trade Processes

According to the World Trade Organization (WTO), shipping company Maersk tracked the paper trail of a shipment of roses and avocados from Kenya to the Netherlands in 2014, finding that it involved about 30 organizations, 200 interactions, 100 people, and 34 days. Largely paper-driven, the global trade system is plagued with multiple requirements, complex documentation flows, and information asymmetry. It is estimated that 30% of the time is spent on processing documents, and $150 billion is lost annually owing to the manual methods in conventional trade finance operations.

The costs and delays associated with onerous documentation woven into a web of regulations are especially too taxing for micro, small, and medium-sized enterprises (MSMEs) to engage in international trade. On top of this, a collateral requirement is typically difficult for many MSMEs to fulfill. A survey conducted by ADB on trade finance gap, growth, and jobs in 2019 revealed that 45% of trade finance applications rejected by banks were from MSMEs. The study also found a $1.5 trillion trade finance gap, which has only grown during the pandemic and adversely affected MSMEs even more.

A report on Trade Financing and COVID-19 by the ICC estimates $1.9 trillion–$5.0 trillion in additional capacity is needed in the trade finance market for a V-shaped recovery from the pandemic. Limited access to finance, coupled with inefficient, costly, and cumbersome paper-heavy trade processes, lowers the economic participation of MSMEs in global trade and limits their job-creating and growth prospects.

Digitalization is critical to closing the finance gap and delivering efficiencies to cross-border activities. Seamless digitalized trade would transform the global economy and make the world more secure through greater transparency and more robust global supply chains. But there are two impediments: the lack of global standards and protocols to drive interoperability and the lack of legislation recognizing digital trade documents.

The lack of standards makes the digital exchange of information difficult and cumbersome, creating fragmentation and inefficiencies in trade. Legislative gaps and legal uncertainty regarding the acceptance of digital trade documentation hinder the transition from paper-heavy to digitalized processes in the global supply chain. Most jurisdictions require negotiable instruments to be in paper form.

A multifaceted approach encompassing regulatory reforms, together with an intergovernmental coordination mechanism, a common framework for leveraging data to better assess financing risk, and a trusted global digital identity system for companies, is key to enabling the transition to digital trade at scale.

Policy Actions

Common international standards

Establishing common international standards allows paperless trade systems to be easily connected, thereby breaking down the digital silos between component parts of the trade ecosystem: exporters, shippers, ports, customs, warehousing, finance, and importers.

Supported by ADB, the ICC Digital Standards Initiative is tasked with advocating the reconciliation of a myriad of standards, rules, and regulations in the global trading system. Central to the initiative is facilitating technical interoperability among both blockchain-based and non-blockchain approaches in the trade space.

Legal recognition of electronic documents and signatures

A strong framework for the legal recognition of electronic documents and signatures is a fundamental step toward global digital trade. The United Nations Commission on International Trade Law (UNCITRAL) has developed the Model Law on Electronic Transferable Records (MLETR) to use these records domestically and across borders by recognizing the legal validity of electronic equivalents of paper-based records. MLETR builds on the principles of nondiscrimination against the use of electronic means, functional equivalence, and technology neutrality, which underpin UNCITRAL texts on e-commerce. It may, therefore, accommodate the use of all technologies and models. The legal recognition and use of electronic transferable records will cause a paradigm shift in international trade by democratizing accessibility to reliable, high-quality, and trusted data.

Intergovernmental coordination mechanism

Through the Framework Agreement on Facilitation of Cross-Border Paperless Trade in Asia and the Pacific (CPTA), the United Nations Economic and Social Commission for Asia and the Pacific (ESCAP) is providing a dedicated intergovernmental framework to develop legal and technical solutions to facilitate cross-border paperless trade among willing member states.

The framework agreement, which took effect on 21 February 2021, is guided by the principles of nondiscrimination, functional equivalence, technological neutrality, and the promotion of interoperability, which are the same general principles supporting UNCITRAL texts, including the MLETR. Therefore, CPTA provides a framework that paves the way for MLETR adoption.

The Association of Southeast Asian Nations (ASEAN) community contributes to the region's digital agenda and trade connectivity through its intergovernmental initiatives and frameworks on e-commerce, data governance, and ASEAN Single Window, among many others. The ASEAN Business Advisory Council leads efforts to connect the digital trade platforms of member states to facilitate seamless trade flows between countries and their key trading partners.

Trade financing for MSMEs

The fundamental issue of MSMEs' access to financing lies in their credit risk profile. Insufficient documentation and poor credit history are obstacles to risk assessment of MSMEs. Lack of collateral and costly due diligence are also factors that deter banks from providing financial support to small businesses.

Distributed ledger technology (e.g., blockchain) can help address these challenges by producing the necessary data for MSMEs. It provides a decentralized, distributed record of transactions, including credit history and commercial disputes. These records are stored in a manner that all parties to the network can trust. Therefore, its data integrity could also streamline the approach to building a global digital identity for MSMEs.

ADB's Trade and Supply Chain Finance Program supports MSMEs, whose ability to trade is impeded by risk perceptions. The program fills market gaps for trade financing by providing guarantees and loans to banks. It works with more than 240 banks in 21 countries to provide companies with the financial support they need to engage in import and export in Asia's most challenging markets. Since 2009, the program has supported more than 33,000 transactions valued at $47.5 billion.

Global digital identity system

Vital for transacting in the modern economy, a digital identity enables participation in online markets and reduces the costs of supplier verification processes, which can be burdensome to MSMEs.

The Global Legal Entity Identifier Foundation (GLEIF), created by the Financial Stability Board, is a nonprofit organization that supports the implementation and use of the Legal Entity Identifier (LEI) code, which can help address anti-money laundering and know-your-customer issues. Global and harmonized, the LEI code is a unique, electronic, 20-digit standard identifier for legal entities based on the International Organization for Standardization (ISO) 17442 standard. Global adoption of LEI can fuel growth in cross-border trade.

Policy Implementation

In collaboration with the International Chamber of Commerce and other key stakeholders, Singapore's Infocomm Media Development Authority (IMDA) developed TradeTrust, an interoperability framework for exchanging digital trade documentation.

Using distributed ledger technology, the TradeTrust framework provides participants with proof of authenticity and origin of documents, enabling a more seamless and efficient flow of goods between digitally interconnected trading partners. It can perform title transfer on trade documents electronically, which is pivotal in digitalizing paper-based processes for cross-border trade.

TradeTrust is currently organized along the following concurrent workstreams to give the network's participants trust and legal certainty regarding exchanged digital documents.

Legal harmonization. Singapore's Electronic Transactions Act was amended to align with the global standard based on the MLETR to provide legal certainty to electronic transactions and legally recognize electronic negotiable instruments within the country's jurisdiction.

Standards development. Singapore has been actively driving and aligning TradeTrust with standards development at the United Nations Centre for Trade Facilitation and Electronic Business and the ISO.

Software components. TradeTrust provides freely available software components and tools under open-source licensing terms that are designed to make it easy for business applications to connect to blockchains to achieve three key functionalities: (i) assure the authenticity of documents, (ii) assure the provenance of documents, and (iii) provide legally valid performance obligation transfers between implementers of the framework.

In November 2020, a TradeTrust trial was launched by IMDA, Singapore Customs, and the Australian Border Force. Electronic certificates of origin were generated in accordance with the TradeTrust framework via the Intergovernmental Ledger system developed by the Australian Border Force and sent to commercial users participating in the trial as well as Singapore Customs for verification. Trial users were asked to give feedback on the multiple verification methods of the TradeTrust framework. This demonstration assured the authenticity and provenance of the files across two independent and unconnected systems (the Intergovernmental Ledger and the TradeTrust Reference Implementation), securing acceptance from regulatory authorities and businesses.

In Thailand, similar efforts are being pursued to boost trade digitization. Leveraging blockchain technology, the National Digital Trade Platform is the country's central system for linking international digital trade data using international standards. The government aims to link the platform with the National Single Window and trade facilitation platforms of other ASEAN and major trade partners. In 2019, the Joint Standing Committee of Commerce, Industry and Banking of Thailand ran a trial of NTDP with participants across various industries. This demonstrated that document processing was faster by 60%.

Efforts on digitalization and paperless trade are also underway in other countries in Asia. Azerbaijan, Bangladesh, Iran, the People's Republic of China, and the Philippines have ratified ESCAP's CPTA, while Armenia and Cambodia have signed it. Other ESCAP member states are in the process of completing their domestic processes for accession.

Recommendations

Pursue digitalization efforts in tandem with the modernization of rules and regulations

Digitalization's multitude of benefits—from traceability to real-time tracking, faster clearance of shipments, prevention of fraud, and reduced compliance costs—cannot be fully realized without an enabling domestic legal environment for electronic transferable records. Countries need to adopt the MLETR and accede to the CPTA, which is designed for member states at all levels of development and digitalization.

Other preconditions for thriving digital markets include consumer protection policies and the cross-border flows of data that underpin e-trade transactions.

Engage stakeholders in the trade ecosystem

An industry-wide collaboration that brings together the private and public sectors and other actors across the value chain is imperative to set the right mix of policies for this new paradigm of trade and ensure that the benefits are shared.

Strengthening supply chains through stakeholder dialogues should include discussions on lessons learned from the pandemic to minimize the scope for future disruptions and to collectively leverage technologies in addressing the fragilities of trade systems and in future-proofing MSMEs, which are the lifeblood of many economies.

Assess gaps and capacity-building needs

As many Asian economies have varying capacities in cross-border paperless trade, they could benefit from ESCAP's Readiness Assessment Guide for Cross-Border Paperless Trade, which can help guide actions at national and agency levels in this area. Countries requiring technical assistance and advisory services on the CPTA could apply for ESCAP's Accession/Ratification Accelerator Programme.

Other policies, such as consumer protection, data governance, and cybersecurity, are important in the digital economy. Therefore, countries also need to reflect on their capacity to design and administer effective regulatory and dispute resolution systems for these matters.

Capacity building for MSMEs should be considered to make them aware of the opportunities offered by digital solutions. Distributed ledger technology and other solutions can help MSMEs access more markets and financing.

Undertake proof of concept and share success stories to secure buy-in

Countries are more inclined to adopt the necessary measures to enable paperless trade when they see examples of use cases and benefits. Participation in trials and other forms of collaboration can help governments and other stakeholders better understand the frameworks and workings of technologies that facilitate digital trade. The experiences of Bahrain and Singapore in adopting MLETR may serve as models for other Asian countries in their digital transformation journey.

Resources

Asian Development Bank (ADB). 2021. *Digitizing Trade in Asia Needs Legislative Reform*. Manila.

Beck, S., et al. 2019. *Trade and the Legal Entity Identifier*. *ADB Briefs*. No. 115. Manila: ADB.

Castellani, L. 2021. Overview of the UNCITRAL Model Law on Electronic Transferrable Records. Presented at the Policy Actions for COVID-19 Economic Recovery Dialogues of the Asian Development Bank. 3 August.

Castellani, L., Loh, S., and Taylor-Digby, L. (moderator). 2020. Joining Forces for Trade Digitisation: SWIFT, the United Nations, and the Singapore Government. SWIFT Sibos webinar. 5 October.

Duangdee, K. 2021. COVID-19 Has Highlighted the Need for Digitizing Trade. Presented at the Policy Actions for COVID-19 Economic Recovery Dialogues of the Asian Development Bank. 3 August.

Ferrarini, B., Maupin, J., and Hinojales, M. 2017. Distributed Ledger Technologies for Developing Asia. *ADB Economics Working Paper Series*. No. 533. Manila: ADB.

Kim, K., et al. 2019. 2019 Trade Finance Gaps, Growth, and Jobs Survey. *ADB Briefs*. No. 113. Manila: ADB.

Kuyler, O. 2021. Digital Standards Initiative. Presented at the Policy Actions for COVID-19 Economic Recovery Dialogues of the Asian Development Bank. 3 August.

Loh, S. Y. 2021. Trade Digitalization—TradeTrust. Presented at the Policy Actions for COVID-19 Economic Recovery Dialogues of the Asian Development Bank. 3 August.

Forging a Path to Recovery through E-Commerce

Le The Phuc
Ministry of Industry and Trade, Viet Nam

Parcel delivery services. E-commerce retailers are enjoying brisk business, but improvements, such as expanding parcel delivery services in rural areas, are needed to support their continued growth (photo by ADB).

Introduction

Viet Nam has made headway in advancing its digital economy, with an internet penetration rate of 70% and roughly 49 million online consumers in 2020. The latest *e-Conomy SEA* report by Google, Temasek, and Bain & Company estimates a 53% growth in the country's e-commerce sector in 2021, despite the shrinking online travel market. It also projects the internet economy to reach $21 billion in 2021, a 31% surge from 2020, and $57 billion by 2025.

Viet Nam's economy has shown resilience relative to its ASEAN neighbors amid the coronavirus disease (COVID-19) pandemic, but it has not been spared from the adverse impact of the crisis. E-commerce will be critical for the nation to forge ahead on its recovery path. Buoyed by a burgeoning tech industry, rising middle class, and growing population of digital natives, its digital economy is poised for considerable growth. To fully reap the dividends of digitalization, Viet Nam should harness e-commerce and prioritize actions rooted in its key enablers: connectivity, digital payments, skills development, logistics systems, cybersecurity, and consumer trust.

Challenges

Although the outlook for the digital economy looks bright, the e-commerce industry is fraught with challenges, particularly in logistics. Compared with other ASEAN countries, Viet Nam faces steep logistics costs, which account for 30%–40% of product sales. Moreover, logistics services are mainly available in big cities, limiting the access of rural consumers to online businesses. Adding to the problems are the lack of qualified personnel and low technology application in logistics.

Another key obstacle to e-commerce is rampant fraud. Online shopping platforms are riddled with counterfeit and low-quality goods, causing customer dissatisfaction and denting their confidence in e-commerce. In the first 9 months of 2020, about 30,000 stores on e-commerce platforms were taken down due to trade fraud, counterfeit, and contraband goods. Consumers with legitimate claims are often left without remedies because of the absence of an official online dispute resolution mechanism in the country. From an intellectual property rights standpoint, there is a need to enhance the legal framework to ensure the authenticity of products and a safe online environment, which could also promote the development of cross-border e-commerce.

When it comes to payments, cash is king in Viet Nam because of the lack of trust in electronic payment (e-payment) and low financial inclusion. The number of unbanked is high in rural areas. While the e-payment ecosystem has grown since the onset of COVID-19, most consumers have a deep-rooted habit of using cash. This discourages large transactions and leads to significant cancellation rates. Such frictions may stymie Viet Nam's progress in e-commerce, which requires an efficient digital payment system.

In terms of digital skills, Viet Nam ranked at the bottom among ASEAN countries in the World Economic Forum's *Global Competitiveness Report* in 2019. In the 2020 Global Talent Competitiveness Index, the country dropped four spots to rank 96th out of 132 countries. Building a talent pipeline depends on the readiness of Vietnamese training institutions for 4IR, which ADB's recent study finds to be generally lower in relation to other ASEAN economies.

Policy Actions for Viet Nam

Develop mechanisms and policies in preparation for 4IR

To realize its goal of becoming one of the top ASEAN countries in e-commerce, Viet Nam needs to modernize its legal and regulatory framework to reflect the new economic realities. Policies and regulations on crucial areas of the internet economy, including cybersecurity, data privacy, and consumer protection, should be regularly reviewed and updated to remain relevant in the ever-evolving digital landscape.

Policies on electronic transactions and data exchange are fundamental to cross-border e-commerce, so Viet Nam must engage in regional cooperation and bilateral agreements to harmonize legislations with other countries and reduce the complexity and cost of digital trade. To this end, Viet Nam's digital economy agreement with Singapore will support alignment of digital trade rules and facilitate interoperability between digital systems. It will encourage collaboration in nascent areas and support the participation of MSMEs in e-commerce. A notable feature of the agreement is its modular approach, which allows flexibility to adapt rules to local conditions where warranted and accommodates countries' varying levels of trade readiness.

A strategic road map could be useful in mainstreaming e-commerce in national development plans as well as in coordinating broader digitalization endeavors. Set with time-bound targets, Viet Nam's National Strategy for Digital Transformation by 2025, Toward 2030 is designed to improve the efficiency of the public sector through the implementation of e-government, narrow the digital gap through infrastructure investments, and bolster economic competitiveness through digital economy. The government has also set a goal for e-commerce training at universities to equip workers with skills aligned with the industry.

In addition, industry associations can play an instrumental role in e-commerce by serving as a coordinating body to bring players from various sectors and influence policymaking. The Viet Nam E-Commerce Association (VECOM), which comprises companies, organizations, and individuals, complements the government's efforts to foster e-commerce in Viet Nam. VECOM serves local firms and MSMEs to enable them to capture opportunities offered by e-commerce.

Build consumer trust and improve capacity to mitigate fraud, infringement of intellectual property rights, and unfair competition

While the upward trend in online shopping is expected to persist, Vietnamese consumers are still wary of engaging in digital transactions due to concerns over security and fraud. Thus, strengthening data governance and privacy laws is becoming highly urgent to raise consumer confidence in e-commerce.

Free trade agreements, such as those between the European Union and Viet Nam and the United Kingdom and Viet Nam as well as the advent of the Regional Comprehensive Economic Partnership, should push Viet Nam to step up its measures on the protection of consumers and intellectual property rights to stop unfair, deceptive, and fraudulent online business practices. Equally important are appropriate enforcement mechanisms and agencies with the right capacity to deal with anticompetitive or fraudulent behaviors in cyberspace. An online dispute resolution system can provide consumers with a fair and timely mechanism for redressing their grievances without undue cost or burden.

Promote e-commerce in provinces and other sectors

VECOM's yearly Viet Nam E-Business Index, which provides e-commerce trends and data across the country, could be leveraged to assess gaps at the subnational level and identify the investment needs for laying the foundation of e-commerce systems in provinces.

Creating a larger market for e-commerce also requires a wider adoption of e-payment. As reflected in its national strategy, Viet Nam's goal is to increase cashless payments to 50% by 2025 and 80% by 2030. Given the high smartphone penetration in the country, mobile money is the most efficient means to expand the use of e-payment, which will facilitate swift and seamless online transactions. This method could be easily deployed in rural and remote areas where the unbanked are largely concentrated.

Finally, digital opportunities in budding sectors should be explored. In the health sector, technological solutions have proven valuable during COVID-19 lockdowns, and further harnessing these tools beyond the pandemic could improve access to quality health care while reducing costs for rural households. In agriculture, strengthening support for farmers to engage online can help them tap into high-value e-commerce markets, thereby boosting agricultural incomes and rural livelihoods overall.

Enhance infrastructure systems and auxiliary services of e-commerce

Information technology (IT) connectivity is the backbone of e-commerce and the digital economy. Viet Nam must further invest in IT infrastructure to become a digital powerhouse. Although great strides to expand internet access have been made, it still needs to provide universal access to 4G networks and invest in 5G mobile networks.

As the market continues to grow, long-term prospects for e-commerce also depend on improving both the hardware and software components of the country's logistics system to meet current and future industry needs. This involves enhancing last-mile connectivity, reliability, and speed of delivery, particularly for low-value or business-to-customer shipments.

General Recommendations

The following policies are recommended for Viet Nam, ASEAN member states, and other economies to promote the development of their e-commerce sector.

Participate in multilateral and bilateral cooperation to harmonize approaches and collectively mitigate challenges

Viet Nam and other economies need to work together to unify rules and laws to enable seamless cross-border electronic trade. ASEAN has been pioneering harmonization of laws, and it is continuously taking stock of progress in e-commerce to identify areas for further alignment and collaboration.

Participation in ASEAN and other regional and global cooperation mechanisms facilitates regulatory coordination on matters that have implications for the digital economy of Viet Nam and the region as a whole. For instance, the cross-border nature of cyberthreats requires cooperation with regional and international parties to respond effectively to growing security risks. As consumers gain more access to international products online, they become more susceptible to cross-border fraudulent practices. Therefore, there is a need to solidify alliances with international partners to better safeguard consumers and build a well-functioning e-commerce system.

Raise awareness to stimulate e-commerce adoption

Although COVID-19 has accelerated the shift to digital technology, educating consumers is still a key component to increasing conversions on e-commerce platforms. It is important to extend knowledge-building activities to governments and entrepreneurs as well. Governments must enrich their knowledge of the constantly changing technologies and trends to ensure that policies remain up to date. As large buyers of goods and services, national and local governments also need to understand better how they can leverage online marketplaces to streamline public procurement.

Governments should lead digital transformation by example. In Viet Nam, the government has set goals to leverage technologies for public service delivery, aiming to achieve a good performance rating on the E-Government Development Index by 2030.

Businesses could benefit from capacity-building activities, including effective advertising and marketing of their brands online, deployment of analytics tools for data-driven decisions to boost sales, and promotion of Vietnamese products in international markets. Amazon's partnership with VECOM, for instance, aims to develop the digital capabilities of local businesses and provide them with the know-how to succeed in e-commerce.

Nurture digital skills and innovation to reap the benefits of digitalization

Rapid digitalization cannot be sustained without technologically savvy and highly skilled workers that can respond and adapt to the digital economy. Recommended measures are to strengthen IT education and training at all levels, partner with the private sector to ensure quality and relevant curricula, and facilitate industry exposure of students through work–study programs. In addition to technical competencies, soft skills should be emphasized to foster agility and resilience, which are essential to thrive in the changing world of work.

Resources

Asian Development Bank. 2021. *Reaping the Benefits of Industry 4.0 through Skills Development in High-Growth Industries in Southeast Asia: Insights from Cambodia, Indonesia, the Philippines, and Viet Nam*. Manila.

Google, Temasek, Bain & Company. 2021. *e-Conomy SEA 2021*. https://services.google.com/fh/files/misc/e_conomy_sea_2021_report.pdf.

Hoa, D. T. P. and L. Chen. 2020. Policy Environment for E-commerce Connectivity in Viet Nam. *E-commerce Connectivity in ASEAN*. Jakarta, Indonesia: Economic Research Institute for ASEAN and East Asia. pp. 120–145.

INSEAD, Google, The Adecco Group. 2020. *The Global Talent Competitiveness Index*.

Phuc, L. T. 2021. Viet Nam's Policies to Facilitate E-Commerce and Digital Transformation. Presented at the Policy Actions for COVID-19 Economic Recovery Dialogues of the Asian Development Bank. 28 September.

Schwab, K., ed. 2019. *The Global Competitiveness Report*. Cologny/Geneva: World Economic Forum.

Viet Nam E-Commerce Association. 2021. *Vietnam E-Business Index 2021 Report*. Ha Noi.

Viet Nam News. 2020. Handling Fake Goods on E-Commerce Platforms. 31 October.

Accelerating E-Commerce in ASEAN

Satvinder Singh
Deputy Secretary-General for ASEAN Economic Community,
Association of Southeast Asian Nations (ASEAN)

Mario Masaya
Digital Policy Director, US–ASEAN Business Council

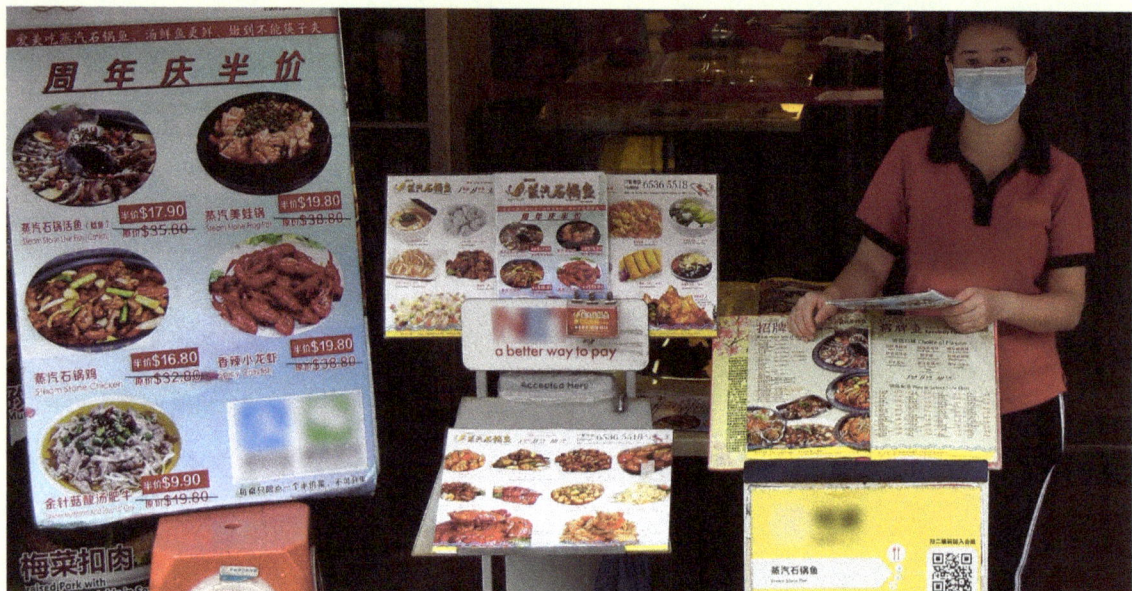

Business in the time of COVID-19. More businesses in Southeast Asia have shifted to contactless digital transactions, such as e-commerce and online payments, to stay open during the pandemic (Photo by ADB).

Introduction

Waves of coronavirus disease (COVID-19) outbreaks have placed populations under a series of lockdowns in different parts of the world. There is greater reliance on digital technologies to keep societies functioning amid disruptions. The use of videoconferencing for virtual work collaboration and apps for buying and selling goods is increasing. Education technologies are being deployed for continued learning. Often viewed in the past as a nice-to-have solution, digital tools have become intrinsic to daily activities.

As illustrated in the 2021 report by Google, Temasek, and Bain & Company, the pandemic has turbocharged the digital transformation of Southeast Asia. Focused on the region's six largest economies—Indonesia, Malaysia, Singapore, Thailand, the Philippines, and Viet Nam—the report's findings show that 40 million people went online for the first time in 2021, bringing the total number of internet users in ASEAN to 440 million, up from 250 million in 2015. They make up 75% of the combined population.

The report sees the size of the region's internet economy to exceed $170 billion in 2021 and reach $360 billion by 2025 and $1 trillion by 2030. Moreover, it notes that nine out of 10 new users from 2020 continue to use digital services this year, demonstrating strong adoption with no signs of reversal. The report also sheds light on the vibrant tech scene in ASEAN, now home to 23 unicorns[4] that play a major role in propelling the region's digital economy.

Despite the favorable trends spawned by this profound online shift, the region's e-commerce ecosystem is beset by a plethora of challenges. While many of these issues predate COVID-19, the need for policy actions has been amplified by the current crisis, drastic changes in the digital landscape, and the new and vital role of e-commerce for individuals and enterprises.

Navigating a New Digital Era

As Southeast Asian countries move forward with their digital transformation and capitalize on e-commerce to bounce back from the crisis, they need to navigate the complexities of a rapidly evolving digital environment and ensure the alignment of their efforts to tackle the multiple facets of this comprehensive agenda.

The past few years have witnessed an alarming surge in cyber risks in the region and across the globe that calls for increased investments in augmenting security. As transactions become increasingly digitalized, the internet has become a fertile ground for crimes. According to INTERPOL's latest ASEAN Cyberthreat Assessment, 7,765 incidents were reported to CyberSecurity Malaysia in the first 8 months of 2020, with fraud topping the list with 5,697 cases. In Indonesia, online fraud was also one of the largest case categories recorded in police reports between January and September 2020. Such incidents can erode the confidence of consumers and businesses to transact online. The ASEAN Digital Integration Index notes that while legislation and regulation of cybersecurity are on track to support digital integration in the region, deficiencies prevail in the implementation of cyberthreat detection systems and in the capability to handle risks.

If emerging online threats, such as data breaches and fraudulent practices, go unheeded, endeavors to expand e-commerce could be undermined. The perceived risks to privacy and security could also increase the reluctance to use e-payment solutions, which are key to facilitating seamless transactions and cross-border trade. Even though the low adoption of digital payment solutions is mainly linked to consumers' traditional reliance on cash, enhancing the security and convenience of cashless methods is imperative to increase their uptake.

At the heart of e-commerce is logistics, whose current framework and customs architecture are designed for the traditional business-to-business model. This creates capacity issues for business-to-consumer shipments. Since digital trade in the region remains nascent, there are still gaps such as deficient infrastructure, lack of integration of logistical networks, weak adoption of international standards for e-trade systems, fragmented or insufficient legal frameworks to recognize digital documents and signatures, and low service capabilities.

---

[4]   Unicorns refer to companies valued at more than $1 billion.

Complicating the preexisting logistical issues is the geographic makeup of some ASEAN countries, such as Indonesia and the Philippines, which face cost and connectivity challenges on last-mile deliveries to remote islands. Often, these far-flung locations have underdeveloped infrastructure and inadequate capacity to participate in e-commerce.

Although the digital economy has overall boomed due to COVID-19, it has also underscored the digital exclusion of rural communities; micro, small, and medium-sized enterprises (MSMEs); and unskilled workers, most of whom are women.

Finally, the exponential rise of e-commerce has come at the expense of the environment. The rising quantities of packaging waste and growing carbon footprint from online deliveries are emerging concerns that need policy attention to ensure that Southeast Asia's digital economy is not only resilient but also sustainable.

Policy Actions

To coordinate efforts to develop e-commerce in ASEAN, the US–ASEAN Business Council proposes policy actions on pivotal issues across the different segments of the e-commerce value chain: the government, private sector, and broader community.

Institutional Measures

- **ASEAN E-Commerce Association and Public–Private E-Commerce Dialogue**
  The growth of e-commerce in ASEAN hinges on a well-coordinated standards and regulatory environment. The proposed ASEAN E-Commerce Association and public–private platform will forge cooperation between actors of the e-commerce ecosystem and facilitate their dialogue on policy measures, reinforcing the regional and national progress made on e-commerce.

Trust and Recognition

- **E-Commerce Trust Mark**
  Transactions are founded on trust, which is difficult to foster in the e-marketplace because of the lack of physical interaction. The ASEAN e-commerce trust mark enables the certification of goods sold online to ensure authenticity, avoid wrongful service descriptions, and strengthen shoppers' confidence. Its implementation can also be an avenue for dispute resolutions, which can help make online shopping safer and fairer.

- **Trusted Trader Scheme**
  A trusted trader scheme can provide accredited ASEAN e-commerce traders with informal clearance, simplified procedures for duty refunds of returned shipments, and lower inspection rates to streamline customs clearance while still adhering to risk mitigation practices. The scheme can be piloted in member states with greater readiness. Once the national schemes are in place in other countries, a mutual recognition agreement that consolidates those schemes can eventually be developed.

- **Technology for Customs**
  Digitalization offers many opportunities to address capacity constraints resulting from the ever-increasing volumes of shipments as well as enhance efficiencies of clearance systems and risk management. However, countries may struggle prioritizing their customs modernization and reforms because they lack know-how and resources. An awareness-building program can help customs officials understand the technology being developed by the private sector that could be applicable to customs procedures to develop proof of concept.

- **Digital ID Framework**
  Widening the acceptance of e-payment solutions can avoid the inherent risks of cash-on-delivery transactions. Cash-dependent economies in Southeast Asia face frictions not only in domestic transactions but also in cross-border trade, which is key to driving post-pandemic recovery.

  Setting up a digital identification framework for ASEAN will help boost the utilization of e-payment methods, mitigate privacy and security threats, and greatly enhance cross-border integration. The latter will require harmonizing regional standards for identification and verification, which will be a long-term undertaking. In the short term, countries could build on the existing national digital ID systems to encourage the adoption of digital financial services by enabling real-time transactions and secure verification of user identities.

Talent, Innovation, and Capacity Building

- **E-Commerce Skills Road Map**
  A critical component of a digital economy is a skilled and trained workforce capable of driving and sustaining digitalization across various functional areas of the ecosystem. Devising a road map in collaboration with the private sector can clarify the skills required for job functions in the e-commerce sector and the appropriate interventions for promoting innovation and ensuring a future-ready workforce.

- **Internship Program**
  Real-world experience through internship programs can cultivate digital literacy in a young workforce. With support from the public and private sectors, industry exposure of students can equip them with the foundational skills and capabilities to thrive in a digital and knowledge-based economy.

- **E-Commerce Awareness-Building Platform**
  Given the dominance of small businesses in ASEAN economies, it is imperative to strengthen their knowledge of technological solutions to enable their e-commerce participation and foster their competitiveness. To fill capacity gaps, the ASEAN SME Academy offers training materials, online courses, and other resources from the region's global business partners, such as Facebook and UPS. A proposed awareness-building platform aims to build on the ASEAN SME Academy by developing local content in various languages.

Seamless Connectivity

- **ASEAN Parcel Locker Network**
  The e-commerce boom has caused last-mile delivery frictions. An interoperable regional locker network for receiving and returning parcels, which may leverage existing physical stores to avoid costs, can ease the last-mile fulfillment challenges and allow consolidated delivery trips to parcel lockers instead of individual residences. An extensive network of parcel lockers should adopt common standards for easy exchange of information and integration of workflows. This generates cost savings from efficient operations for logistics providers and promotes environmental sustainability through reduced vehicle traffic.

- **ASEAN Low Value Shipment Program**
  The ASEAN Low Value Shipment Program, where customs procedures are simplified, would help address concerns on complex customs rules felt primarily by MSMEs. Based on the World Customs Organization's Immediate Release Guidelines, the program focuses on streamlining the clearance process for low-value goods, which currently receive the same degree of scrutiny as high-value shipments.

- **ASEAN E-Commerce Land Connectivity Pilot**
  To take advantage of efficiency gains and cost savings from cross-border trucking, the proposed pilot would allow the transportation and distribution of goods between city pairs using the ASEAN Highway Network. It will comprise eligible long-haul feeders qualifying for pre-clearance and the use of a green lane at checkpoints, thereby optimizing supply chains, improving time in transit, reducing emissions, and lowering costs.

E-Commerce Cooperation

Recognizing the significance of e-commerce in regional economic integration, ASEAN has undertaken efforts to accelerate this sector through intergovernmental mechanisms and frameworks. In 2017, the ASEAN Coordinating Committee on Electronic Commerce was established. In 2018, it developed the ASEAN Digital Integration Framework to put together various digital initiatives to support e-commerce transactions across the region. With the signing of the ASEAN Agreement on E-Commerce in 2019, ASEAN set up the basic structure underpinning its digital economy, including the digital infrastructure, legal and regulatory environment, payment systems, data governance, consumer protection, competition, cybersecurity, and digital skills.

The seismic shifts in the ASEAN digital scene have prompted initiatives to keep pace with the fast-moving advancements in the region. In January, the ASEAN Digital Master Plan 2021–2025 was adopted. In September, the 53rd ASEAN Economic Ministers' Meeting endorsed the Work Plan on the Implementation of ASEAN Agreement on E-commerce 2021–2025, which provides a balanced approach for countries to realize the value of the agreement across the key focus areas of cross-border connectivity, business, and consumer. The ASEAN economic ministers also endorsed the Bandar Seri Begawan Roadmap: An ASEAN Digital Transformation Agenda to Accelerate ASEAN's Economic Recovery and Digital Economy Integration, which provides a visionary direction to accelerate pandemic recovery efforts while laying the groundwork for negotiating the ASEAN Digital Economy Framework Agreement in 2025.

In addition, e-commerce forms part of the ASEAN Comprehensive Recovery Framework, specifically under Broad Strategy 4 on Accelerating Inclusive Digital Transformation. The strategy aims to seize digital transformation and opportunities presented by digital technologies to boost the ASEAN economy and improve society in the post-COVID-19 world.

Last, the inclusion of e-commerce provisions in the largest trade agreement, the Regional Comprehensive Economic Partnership, is a welcome development. The e-commerce chapter of the Regional Comprehensive Economic Partnership focuses on the adoption of digitized solutions, establishment of legal frameworks for paperless trading and data protection, and cooperation between ASEAN and other member states on cybersecurity and other critical enablers of e-commerce.

Recommendations

Establish a holistic road map through multilayer cooperation

Managing the swift developments in the e-commerce ecosystem while advancing the vision of a single market requires a balanced set of policy measures informed by key stakeholders from various levels of the public and private sectors in ASEAN. Their collective efforts are crucial to establishing links between the virtual and physical elements of digital commerce, whose growth is contingent on essential preconditions such as a conducive legal and regulatory framework for digital trade documentation, interoperable systems based on common standards, consumer protection, cybersecurity, and data-sharing across governments and businesses based on international best practices.

Multi-stakeholder support is also needed to help the ASEAN Secretariat reinforce its statistical system and enhance its research capacity to better monitor, evaluate, and coordinate regional efforts in carrying forward the e-commerce and digital transformation agenda.

Foster an inclusive and equitable digital economy

For everyone to benefit from e-commerce, governments must address systemic connectivity challenges by expanding affordable and quality broadband in rural and underserved areas. However, technology and connectivity alone will not be sufficient to address the digital divide. Capacity-building activities are necessary to realize the full advantages of the digital economy. Resources for supporting MSMEs to access new markets and reduce the barriers to their technology adoption as well as enhance digital literacy among women, poor people, and vulnerable groups can help create a more inclusive economy in the modern era. Also important are efforts to ensure fair competition to avoid the concentration of market power and bring adequate choices for consumers.

For economies with limited capacities for cross-border paperless trade, the *Readiness Assessment Guide for Cross-Border Paperless Trade* of the United Nations Economic and Social Commission for Asia and the Pacific (ESCAP) may serve as a useful resource to design policy actions.

Inject circularity into e-commerce

The e-commerce boom serves as an opportunity to transition the retail industry and consumption patterns to sustainable practices. Given the emerging consumer preference for quality products with environmental and social considerations, there should be greater collaboration between online shopping platforms and sustainability-oriented merchants. Similar partnerships can be established with logistics service providers through joint efforts to green and optimize the supply chain.

Finally, the ASEAN community could explore the measures being assessed by the European Union in line with its European Green Deal, such as sustainable trade options in the form of refurbished products to cater to green consumerism.

Resources

Facebook and Bain & Company. 2021. Southeast Asia, The Home For Digital Transformation. *SYNC Southeast Asia*. 30 August.

Google, Temasek, Bain & Company. 2021. *e-Conomy SEA 2021*. https://services.google.com/fh/files/misc/e_conomy_sea_2021_report.pdf.

INTERPOL. 2021. *ASEAN Cyberthreat Assessment 2021*. Singapore.

Masaya, M. 2021. *A Vision for Cross-Border E-Commerce in ASEAN*. Presented at the Policy Actions for COVID-19 Economic Recovery Dialogues of the Asian Development Bank. 28 September.

Singh, S. 2021. Policy Options for Accelerating E-Commerce in the New Normal. Presented at the Policy Actions for COVID-19 Economic Recovery Dialogues of the Asian Development Bank. 28 September.

US–ASEAN Business Council. 2021. *A Vision for Cross-Border E-Commerce in ASEAN*.

CHAPTER 3
Accelerating Green Recovery,
Clean Energy, and Circular
Economy Transitions

Green Policies for Post-COVID-19 Economic Recovery in Southeast Asia

Anouj Mehta
Country Director of Thailand Resident Mission
Asian Development Bank

Wind turbines and solar panels. The Asian Development Bank-supported Green Recovery Program bridges the financing gap for green infrastructure, such as clean energy production, in Southeast Asia (photo by ADB).

Introduction

The Association of Southeast Asian Nations (ASEAN) member states need to scale up green infrastructure. Investing in infrastructure is critical to enhancing connectivity in Southeast Asia and vital in reducing poverty and achieving development outcomes. While infrastructure is the backbone of economic growth in the region, its environmental costs remain particularly high.

The Asian Development Bank (ADB) estimates that Southeast Asia will require $210 billion per year from 2016 to 2030 to support investment in vital climate-resilient infrastructure. Prior to the coronavirus disease (COVID-19) pandemic, infrastructure investment, particularly from private capital sources, was far below the levels required. Taking climate change into account, ADB estimates the investment gap to be 3.8%–4.1% of the gross domestic product (GDP) from 2016 to 2020 in select ASEAN countries.

COVID-19 had a major impact in Southeast Asia, with economic contraction at 4.0% in 2020 based on ADB estimates. Post-COVID-19 policies and investments need to achieve socioeconomic and environmental outcomes to enhance the sustainability and resilience of economies in the medium to long term. Pursuing a green recovery will be critical to ensure an environmentally resilient future in Southeast Asia.

Why a Green Recovery?

The United Nations Sustainable Development Goals (SDGs) report for 2020 estimates that around 71 million people were pushed back into extreme poverty in 2020, confirming the scope and scale of setbacks for achieving the SDGs worldwide.

Meanwhile, individual country contributions submitted to date would only cut about 1% of global greenhouse gas (GHG) emissions—a far cry from the 45% cut needed by 2030 to meet the 1.5-degrees Celsius goal set by the Intergovernmental Panel on Climate Change.

The 10 ASEAN member states have all ratified the Paris Agreement under the United Nations Framework Convention on Climate Change (Paris Agreement) and committed to their nationally determined contributions (NDCs). They already set a target of generating 23% of their primary energy from renewable sources by 2025. A comparison between expected emissions that would occur by meeting NDC targets and the emission targets needed to meet Paris goals reveals an estimated gap of 415 metric tons of carbon dioxide equivalent ($mtCO_2e$). This means that emissions need to be reduced by an additional 11%. According to the Green Climate Fund, NDC targets in the ASEAN region remain highly dependent on external investment and support.

Globally, investors are calling on governments to implement green recovery plans. While significant progress has been made in Southeast Asia to scale up green infrastructure prior to the pandemic, the COVID-19 crisis has slowed down the momentum of climate action. Resource allocations originally intended for climate action had to be redirected as public budgets faced increasing pressure and private investments took the back seat. Clear and robust low-carbon policies and green national recovery strategies are needed to reduce the risk of future pandemics, mitigate and adapt to the impact of climate change, and improve competitiveness. Green policies and strategies will also guide investors, businesses, workers, and consumers toward sustainability, such as through frameworks for sustainable finance and taxonomy principles.

A green recovery approach from the COVID-19 crisis is crucial for four reasons:
   (i) Safeguard the environment to enhance resilience against future pandemics.
   (ii) Address the worsening impacts of climate change and biodiversity loss and their economic consequences.
   (iii) Boost economies through green stimulus policies (as demonstrated in past crises).
   (iv) Strengthen Southeast Asia's long-term economic competitiveness through a green recovery approach.

Policy Options

Countries recognize the need to create longer-term economic recovery packages to address the challenges and mitigate the risks brought about by the pandemic. This involves balancing economic growth with safeguarding natural capital. The three pillars to balance green recovery strategies are the following:

(i)   Leverage scarce government funds as best as possible.

(ii) Mitigate heightened project risk perception to catalyze private finance.

(iii) Accelerate protection of natural resources and climate resilience.

In designing green recovery strategies, governments can consider nine policy levers to influence significant environmental outcomes:

1. **Pricing of externalities.** Put a price on environmental externalities of activities to influence market decisions (e.g., carbon taxes).

2. **Financial support for green products and services.** Provide loans and grants for products and services with environmental impacts (e.g., energy-efficiency retrofits in the construction sector), disburse public funds to private corporations after environmental actions are taken, and promote green public procurement.

3. **Catalyzing private sector financing.** Mobilize private sector investments in areas with environmental implications (e.g., green financing approaches).

4. **Public investments in supporting infrastructure.** Invest in projects with specific environmental outcomes (e.g., renewable energy projects, responsible mining activities).

5. **Support for innovation.** Finance the development of new technologies with environmental implications (e.g., research and development for electric vehicle deployment).

6. **Addressing non-price market failures.** Impose environmental standards and regulations (e.g., property rights) in specific industries or activities with environmental impacts or their reversal (deregulation).

7. **Behavioral change and skills development programs.** Trigger behavioral changes (e.g., "nudge" policies to alter consumer preferences toward sustainability) and create skills programs to build capacity for green projects (e.g., regenerative agricultural techniques).

8. **New collaborations.** Foster collaborations within or between industries and other actors (government, civil society, etc.) to influence environmental outcomes.

9. **New information systems.** Address information asymmetries by alerting businesses to risks, providing information to consumers, and driving transparency in environmental performance.

Three Steps toward a Green Recovery

Implementing a green recovery in Southeast Asia requires three key steps or policy actions:

Step 1: Build mechanisms to produce a lasting shift toward ecosystem resilience.

There are four mechanisms that policy makers can use to incorporate green objectives into government policies:

(i) Develop a more integrated approach toward green growth, working across government agencies to assess trade-offs or possible shared benefits of green policies pursued by different agencies.

(ii) Assess all policy interventions with a green lens.

(iii) Build a rigorous approach to data collection and target setting.

(iv) Ensure government agencies have the right skills to execute a green growth agenda.

Step 2: Implement targeted policy interventions focused on five areas of opportunity.

There are five green growth opportunities in areas that are most relevant for Southeast Asia.

(i) Productive and regenerative agriculture

(ii) Sustainable urban development and transport models

(iii) Clean energy transition

(iv) Circular economy models

(v) Healthy and productive oceans

If leveraged fully, these five areas will require $172 billion in capital investment and can create 30 million jobs in Southeast Asia by 2030. These opportunities can also help toward meeting the SDGs.

Step 3: Identify sustainable sources of financing.

Governments must determine at the outset how they will finance investments in these five areas. Options include collecting green taxes (e.g., carbon taxes), removing brown subsidies (e.g., fossil fuel subsidies), mobilizing private sector finance (e.g., green finance catalytic facilities and sustainable impact bonds), and leveraging international finance sources. In particular, Southeast Asian countries can use the ASEAN Catalytic Green Finance Facility to acquire sovereign loans and technical assistance for green infrastructure projects on sustainable transport, clean energy, and resilient water systems.

Regional and Country Strategies

Support for a green recovery approach is evident in regional strategies. The ASEAN Comprehensive Recovery Framework emphasizes environmental sustainability as a key component of the region's post-pandemic economic recovery process. The Greater Mekong Subregion COVID-19 Response and Recovery Plan 2021–2023 focuses on developing healthy cities, crops, livestock, and communities as part of its overall strategy to enhance resilience against future pandemics.

Southeast Asian countries have also developed their own policy responses.

The Philippines continues to spend efforts in mobilizing financing for green and sustainable projects. These efforts include:

- establishing the interagency technical working group on sustainable finance (CCC Resolution No. 2021-002),
- developing the Sustainable Finance Roadmap,
- developing the NDC Financial Plan,
- developing Green and Sustainable Bonds Standards (SEC Memorandum Circular No. 8), and
- establishing Sustainable Finance Framework (BSP Circular No. 1085).

Implemented policies in the Philippines include the following:

- First NDC: Cumulative economy-wide GHG emission reduction and avoidance from the business-as-usual scenario of 75% (2.71% unconditional, 72.29% condition).
- Moratorium for Greenfield Coal-Fired Projects: New planned coal projects will no longer receive permits from the Department of Energy.

Thailand is committed to dealing with climate change following the Paris Agreement and supporting the SDGs. Through its Ministry of Finance, Thailand issued a benchmark bond series under its Sustainable Financing Framework, accessing the capital markets for a post-COVID-19 green recovery in August 2020. It is one of the first such sovereign bonds globally that combine green and social impacts with COVID-19 recovery. The bond was oversubscribed three times, and its proceeds will be used to finance green infrastructure and social projects supporting the country's COVID-19 recovery and SDGs 3 and 8, including public health care and employment generation. It will fund Bangkok's Mass Rapid Transit Orange Line (East) Project, which was certified as low-carbon transport by the Climate Bonds Standards and Certification Scheme.

ADB's commitment to helping Southeast Asia shape a climate-resilient and environmentally sustainable economic recovery from the COVID-19 pandemic includes the ACGF-managed Green Recovery Program, which provides technical assistance and concessional loans to about 25 green infrastructure projects across Southeast Asia in key sectors, such as sustainable transport, renewable energy and energy-efficient systems, and low-carbon agriculture and natural resources.

Policy Recommendations

Some crosscutting policy recommendations to implement a green recovery include the following:

Subsidy reform and carbon pricing. Thailand's Climate Change Master Plan 2015–2050 intends to use taxes to curb carbon emissions and an emissions trading market as policy tools to reduce GHG emissions in 2030 to 20.8%, which is below the business-as-usual levels.

Similarly, Indonesia implemented subsidy reforms in 2015 to remove fuel subsidies for gasoline and diesel, saving the government Rp211 trillion ($15.6 billion) or 10% of all government expenditures.

Accelerate research and innovation in green technologies. Thailand's Climate Change Master Plan 2015–2050 identified adaptation and risk management for water, agriculture, and energy sectors as areas to develop an enabling environment for climate change management. Beyond the environmental benefits, the Global Green Growth Institute, for example, estimated that incorporating green technologies to enhance circularity in four industries in Cambodia (garments, food and beverage processing, electronics manufacturing, and brick manufacturing) could translate into increased GDP contributions of between 14.7% (for brick manufacturing) and 35.5% (for electronics) and create 512,000 jobs.

Gender-specific entrepreneurship programs for green opportunities. The United Nations Development Programme's Women's Green Business Initiative addresses existing structural barriers to women's economic advancement and facilitates equal opportunities for them to participate in the green economy.

Green finance

The main policy recommendations focusing on green finance, the author's core area of expertise, to bridge the bankability gap and achieve an effective green economic recovery in the region are the following:

- Encourage access to green funds by increasing the amount of concessional funds and incentivizing green investments from the public and private sectors.

- Develop and promote capacity building programs on green and innovative finance approaches to help countries identify dark green projects and financially structure them to attract private capital and create innovative bankable models, which will be key to developing green project pipelines.

- Create new catalytic facilities at the national level and/or regional level that can transition green infrastructure projects across the bankability gap, hence attracting private finance (e.g., SDG Indonesia One—Green Finance Facility, under the ASEAN Catalytic Green Finance Facility), and mainstream new innovative finance instruments (e.g., SDG Accelerator Bond).

Resources

AlphaBeta. 2021. Policy Advice for COVID-19 Economic Recovery in Southeast Asia: Green Recovery.

Alvarez, P. S. 2021. Mobilizing Finance for Green Projects in the Philippines. Presented at the Policy Actions for COVID-19 Economic Recovery Dialogues of the Asian Development Bank. 8 July.

Asian Development Bank (ADB). ASEAN Catalytic Green Finance Facility (ACGF).

_____. 2020. ASEAN Catalytic Green Finance Facility: Operations Plan 2019–2021. Manila.

_____. 2020. Green Finance Strategies for Post-COVID-19 Economic Recovery in Southeast Asia: Greening Recoveries for Planet and People. Manila.

_____. 2021. Accelerating Sustainable Development after COVID-19: The Role of SDG Bonds. Manila.

_____. 2021. ASEAN Catalytic Green Finance Facility 2019–2020: Accelerating Green Finance in Southeast Asia. Manila.

_____. 2021. Asian Development Outlook 2021: Financing a Green and Inclusive Recovery. Manila.

_____. 2021. Implementing a Green Recovery in Southeast Asia. ADB Briefs. No. 173. Manila.

Government of Thailand, Ministry of Natural Resources and Environment. 2015. Climate Change Masterplan 2015–2020. https://climate.onep.go.th/wp-content/uploads/2019/07/CCMP_english.pdf.

Green Climate Fund. 2021. FP156. ASEAN Catalytic Green Finance Facility (ACGF): Green Recovery Program.

Hutachareon, P. 2021. Green Policies for Post-COVID-19 Economic Recovery. Presented at the Policy Actions for COVID-19 Economic Recovery Dialogues of the Asian Development. 8 July.

International Institute for Sustainable Development. 2016. Indonesia Uses Savings from Fossil Fuel Subsidy Reform to Finance Development. https://www.iisd.org/articles/press-release/indonesia-uses-savings-fossil-fuel-subsidy-reform-finance-development. Press release. 13 June.

Mehta, A. 2021. Mainstream Green Finance. Presented at the Policy Actions for COVID-19 Economic Recovery Dialogues of the Asian Development Bank. 8 July.

United Nations. 2020. The Sustainable Development Goals Report 2020.

United Nations Development Programme. 2015. Women's Green Business Initiative. https://www.undp.org/sites/g/files/zskgke326/files/publications/Womens-Green-Business.pdf.

Powering the Clean Energy Transition

Pradeep Tharakan
Director, Energy Transition, Sectors Group
Asian Development Bank

Hydropower plant. A hydropower plant in the Lao People's Democratic Republic exports electricity to Thailand (photo by ADB).

Introduction

The coronavirus disease (COVID-19) pandemic slowed down development progress globally, but climate change has only accelerated. In Southeast Asia, typhoons, flooding, and drought have become more common, intense, destructive, and increasingly costly. Being highly vulnerable to the impacts of climate change, the region must not only adapt to weather extremes and rising sea levels but also speed up reductions in carbon emissions.

Historically, Southeast Asia's greenhouse gas (GHG) emissions have been low compared with those of advanced economies. However, it has one of the world's fastest-growing rates of emissions, second only to South Asia, because of excessive reliance on fossil fuels.

If left unmanaged, the current emissions trajectory will bring far-ranging environmental, economic, and social repercussions, affecting many lives. The World Health Organization (WHO) says more than a third of the 7 million premature deaths linked to air pollution annually occur in Southeast Asia. The upswing in GHG could lead to a temperature rise beyond the 1.5-degree limit, which will unleash more severe consequences. Thus, the region must decouple its economic growth from fossil fuels. A critical aspect across many net-zero pathways is reducing the power sector's carbon intensity in the near to medium term since other sectors, such as transport and industry, will take much longer to decarbonize.

Power Shift: Problems and Prospects

While the pandemic led to substantial economic contraction, emissions fell modestly and are expected to rebound to pre-pandemic levels as economic activities gather pace. In Southeast Asia, energy demand is rising considerably in line with economic growth, demographic expansion, and rapid urbanization. A key driver of power consumption is the use of air conditioning, which is expected to surge as incomes and temperatures rise.

The abundance of solar, wind, biomass, geothermal, and hydro resources in the region presents vast opportunities for tapping clean energy sources. The region has been ramping up its renewable power generation capacity, which reached 86.7 gigawatts (GW) in 2020, according to the International Renewable Energy Agency (IRENA). It is targeting a 23% share of renewable energy in its total primary energy supply and 35% in its installed power capacity by 2025. Attaining these targets requires countries to step up renewable energy expansion as well as transmission grid upgrades to absorb large-scale deployment of variable energy.

The region, however, remains a hot spot for coal given its low cost and indigenous supply. In addition to the region's nearly 80 GW of operating coal-fired power plants, several more are in the pipeline. It is worrying that some countries still use subsidies to support the coal sector, undermining the competitive position of clean technologies.

Many Southeast Asian economies have made net-zero pledges, yet their climate targets fall short of mitigating the serious threats they face. Coastal populations are vulnerable to extreme weather conditions, and some parts of the region are already sinking, with many livelihoods exposed to the mounting frequency and intensity of climate hazards. Swift and stronger mitigation and adaptation measures are urgently needed.

Policy Prescriptions

Create an enabling environment for a clean energy transition

Governments play a vital role in overcoming barriers to and creating enabling conditions for a clean energy transition, ensuring efficient and effective planning, and encouraging new market players and alternative business models.

Developing a robust framework for the shift to renewables includes sound power development plans, long-term decarbonization strategies, resource assessments, and road maps for an equitable transition. As the financing needed to usher in this transition is massive, governments must create a conducive environment for private investments in transmission and distribution grid upgrades and storage systems. Carbon financing instruments and climate finance could also bridge the huge financing gap by redirecting investments to clean technologies and encouraging energy efficiency.

Enable energy efficiency at scale

Coping with growth in energy demand requires supply-side interventions complemented by demand-side efficiency improvements. While countries in the region have developed energy efficiency programs—including regulatory requirements; information provision; and a combination of economic, financial, and fiscal incentives—some are lax in enforcing their standards. This highlights the need for regional harmonization to scale up energy efficiency and facilitate the trade of more efficient technologies.

It is also vital to support the development of energy service companies, which design, build, and arrange financing for projects that save energy, reduce energy costs, and decrease operation and maintenance costs at their customers' facilities.

Enable and expand access to green finance

Meeting the region's 2025 target of 23% renewables in the primary energy supply requires an estimated annual investment of $27 billion (IRENA). Investments of a much higher scale will be needed to attain net-zero emission targets by mid-century. Public sector funding alone is insufficient to fill the funding challenge, which has become more acute in the wake of the pandemic. Financial instruments have evolved (e.g., thematic bonds, blended finance, green and climate funds) and expanded to unlock various sources of capital for sustainability-oriented investments, including renewable energy. One tool, the transition bond, is designed to support "brown" companies in carbon-intensive or heavily polluting sectors in their shift to green or environmentally sustainable modes of operation.

Recognizing the financing shortfall for climate action and green infrastructure, ADB launched the ASEAN Catalytic Green Finance Facility (ACGF) in 2019. The ACGF provides ASEAN members with technical assistance and access to over $1 billion in loans from cofinancing partners. It focuses on projects that promote renewable energy, energy efficiency, sustainable urban transport, water supply and sanitation, waste management, and climate-resilient agriculture.

Enhance regional power trade

In the face of skyrocketing oil and gas prices, countries must prioritize energy security and resilience. Reorienting power systems toward renewable energy and regional connectivity can reduce dependence on fossil fuel imports, allow for better management of intermittent renewables by accessing flexible resources, and lower the risk of curtailment by providing access to greater and diverse regional demand across countries.

The Lao People's Democratic Republic–Thailand–Malaysia–Singapore Power Integration is currently the only multicountry power trade project operating in the region. Intergovernmental platforms, including the ASEAN Power Grid initiative and the GMS Regional Power Trade Coordination Committee, are facilitating discussions on greater integration of power systems.

ADB has been exploring opportunities for cross-border interconnections and power development planning in the region through its series of technical assistance activities and by providing financing for priority projects. Through ADB's support, the GMS Transmission and Generation Masterplan was developed, and capacity-building activities for country energy and environmental planning agencies and utilities have been conducted across the region.

Support accelerated retirement and repurposing of fossil fuel-based power generation assets

Accelerating the retirement of coal-fired power plant capacity is essential for decarbonizing regional power systems. ADB is developing the Energy Transition Mechanism (ETM) as a market-based approach to accelerate the transition from fossil fuels to clean energy. The initiative is being piloted in Indonesia, the Philippines, and Viet Nam. It will mobilize the public and the private sectors—governments, multilateral banks, private sector investors, philanthropies, and long-term investors—to finance country-specific ETM funds that will seek to retire coal power assets earlier than if they remained with their current owners.

Support clean energy deployment as an economic recovery tool

With the worsening impacts of climate change, a clean energy transition should be central to COVID-19 recovery programs in the region. Investing in clean energy infrastructure has resulted in a larger increase in local jobs and local economic benefits than investments in fossil fuels. And according to an IRENA study, 32% of workers in renewable energy are women, compared with only 22% in the oil and gas industry.

Raise the ambition of climate policies and expand global cooperation

Climate change is a daunting development challenge that transcends borders. It, therefore, calls for greater global consensus and cooperation along with bold targets to tackle its widespread and multidimensional consequences. With the stark divides in resources and emissions contributions, equity must be at the core of a comprehensive international response. Wealthy and high-emitting nations must support the mitigation and adaptation needs of developing countries, which have historically contributed the least to climate change yet suffer disproportionately from its impacts. Given the unprecedented capital required for climate action, additional financing can be mobilized by leveraging Southeast Asia's position in international negotiations.

From Pledge to Progress

Countries in the region have taken significant strides in embracing clean energy.

In Cambodia, a national solar park with a 100-megawatt capacity was developed with technical and financial assistance from ADB. This pathbreaking public–private partnership transaction catalyzed the rollout of more solar photovoltaic projects in the country, resulting in record-low prices. From 2016 to 2021, solar power generation capacity grew from practically none to 377 megawatts, representing 12% of the total installed capacity. ADB is also helping the country expand the market for energy-efficient technologies by establishing a policy and regulatory framework for energy efficiency and upgrading infrastructure with more energy-efficient equipment, materials, and designs.

As a production powerhouse with soaring energy demand, Viet Nam has capitalized on opportunities in renewables, becoming the first mover in floating solar and demonstrating success in rooftop solar, contributing to 48% of its solar capacity in 2020. It also boasts favorable conditions for wind power, with installed capacity expected to grow to more than 20 GW by 2045. However, the grid infrastructure has not been able to keep up with the rapid growth of renewables, resulting in production losses. To meet the demand for a sustainable and stable transmission system, the government amended the Law on Electricity to promote the involvement of private investors in constructing the transmission grid. Moreover, Viet Nam's Power Development Plan 8, which incorporates its net-zero ambition by 2050, aims to have no new coal-fired power plants except those already under construction or planned for completion by 2025 or sooner and prioritize natural gas power projects over coal.

In Indonesia, the strategy to achieve carbon neutrality by 2060 includes increasing the installed capacity for renewables, promoting the use of energy-efficient technologies and electric vehicles and stoves, deploying smart grids to manage intermittent renewable energy, halting approval of new coal plants after 2023, and accelerating the retirement of coal-fired power plants with support from ADB's ETM and other sources.

A key element of the Philippines' decarbonization plan is reducing coal power plants in its energy sector. In 2020, the government announced a moratorium on new coal plants and collaborated with ADB on the ETM. The country's climate agenda is underpinned by its Sustainable Finance Roadmap, which aims to spur green and climate investments from various sources.

Recommendations

Take a programmatic approach to secure better coordination and sustained impact

The clean energy transition entails a series of interlinked actions, from setting clear plans and enabling policies to develop project investment pipelines and forging partnerships that deliver concurrently on these key imperatives: access to renewable energy, energy efficiency, and coal phaseout.

Common limiting factors, such as the inadequate capacity of the grid infrastructure, should be part of planning to avoid project delays. The pathway to net zero can also strongly benefit from multi-stakeholder coordination at the local, national, and international levels, facilitating speedy project design and implementation and access to low-cost financing.

Consider competitive tendering for optimal pricing

Some Southeast Asian countries are increasingly introducing local content requirements to spur local job creation, develop domestic production, and promote technology transfer. However, their imposition can lead to reduced competition and efficiency losses. On the other hand, a global auction scheme facilitates transparency and lowers costs through a competitive process. A phased approach with competitive bidding followed by progressively requiring more local content could help pave the way for a rapid scale-up of low-cost renewables while building local industry in the medium term.

Build resilience through adaptation investments and regional connectivity

In tandem with decarbonization efforts, countries need to reduce their exposure to the worsening global warming impacts and increasing physical climate risks by building a more resilient energy infrastructure. Regional power trade can foster resilience and energy security. It helps improve reliability and increase the share of and synergies among clean energy resources, thereby insulating economies from fossil fuel price shocks.

Account for just transition activities in the mobilization of climate finance

Beyond infrastructure investments, funds must be mobilized to deal with the socioeconomic impacts of the clean energy transition. In light of the COVID-19 crisis, a green recovery and support for vulnerable groups must go hand in hand. Thus, assessing resource needs for climate action should consider investments in reskilling affected workers and communities, as well as support for small enterprises to help them seize new opportunities in the green economy.

Resources

Aleluia, J. et al. 2022. Accelerating a Clean Energy Transition in Southeast Asia: Role of Governments and Public Policy. *Renewable and Sustainable Energy Reviews*. 159 (112226).

Alvarez, P. S. 2022. Accelerating Clean Energy Transition in the Philippines. Presented at the Policy Actions for COVID-19 Economic Recovery Dialogues of the Asian Development Bank. 20 April.

IRENA. 2018. *Renewable Energy Market Analysis: Southeast Asia*. Abu Dhabi.

Misna, A. 2022. NRE Development towards Net-Zero Emission. Presented at the Policy Actions for COVID-19 Economic Recovery Dialogues of the Asian Development Bank. 20 April.

Nguyen, A. 2022. Viet Nam Energy Sector: Success and Lessons Learned in Clean Energy Transition. Presented at the Policy Actions for COVID-19 Economic Recovery Dialogues of the Asian Development Bank. 20 April.

Tharakan, P. 2022. Accelerating Clean Energy Transition in the New Normal. Presented at the Policy Actions for COVID-19 Economic Recovery Dialogues of the Asian Development Bank. 20 April.

A Systems Approach for Transitioning Southeast Asia to a Circular Economy

James Baker

Senior Circular Economy Specialist (Plastic Wastes), Climate Change and Sustainable Development Department, Asian Development Bank

Garbage problem. Circular systems can help cities address their growing garbage problem through upstream (before consumption) and downstream (after disposal) waste management (photo by ADB).

Introduction

The current trajectory of Southeast Asia's production and consumption resulting from its rapid growth is increasingly putting a strain on the environment. Measures to contain the pandemic have intensified the environmental pressures because of increasing volumes of medical waste, plastics, and packaging due to the e-commerce boom, and other resource stresses.

As countries in the region embark on their green recovery agenda in the wake of coronavirus disease (COVID-19), there is a pressing need to transition from the linear economic model of "take, make, waste" to a circular system. A circular economy is grounded in three principles: (i) designing out waste and reducing pollution, (ii) keeping products and materials in use, and (iii) regenerating natural ecosystems. According to a study by the Economic Research Institute for ASEAN and East Asia, this paradigm shift can bring about economic growth of $324 billion and create 1.5 million jobs in Asia by 2025.

Although the term "circular economy" may not yet be commonplace in policy-making circles, countries in the region were already introducing various pertinent policies and regulations as far back as the 1990s and early 2000s. However, approaches were fragmented across the region. Given Southeast Asia's strong economic integration, it is imperative to foster coherence in this area by formulating and coordinating circular economic policies at the regional level.

An Ambitious Agenda

Linear approaches are deeply rooted in our systems and heavily integrated into our communities, economies, and national development. The transition to a circular economy is an ambitious agenda, requiring not only innovative technologies but also massive capital and new business models coupled with significant behavioral changes.

While circularity has gained traction over the years, the lack of a regulatory framework and incentives inhibits implementation. In some jurisdictions, recycling and reusing materials may hinder pushing circular models due to hygiene and consumer protection laws. In addition, the lack of standards for recycled and remanufactured products may lead to variations in the quality and performance of such goods.

Engaging in a circular economy strategy may also bring difficult trade-offs. For instance, imposing extended producer responsibility can cause suppliers to leave small markets. There may be options on the consumer side to shift to circular consumption patterns, but these may be considered impractical and inconvenient. Consumer acceptance is a critical factor in scaling circularity, and this could be influenced by the quality of recycled goods and other circular innovations and perception of secondhand or upcycled products.

ASEAN Framework for a Circular Economy

ASEAN has developed a framework highlighting the role of trade, technological innovations, and financial markets in accelerating circular transformation. The following are its five strategic priorities, which set a path for the smooth transition to a circular economy.

Harmonization of standards and mutual recognition of circular products and services. ASEAN countries must review existing arrangements in various sectors and harmonize standards to enable the trade of circular products and services and facilitate integration between value chains. To mainstream and scale circularity, ASEAN countries should establish a broadly accepted definition of circular products and services by developing a taxonomy, which can help minimize the cost of compliance among businesses and reduce unnecessary regulatory burdens.

Trade openness and trade facilitation in goods and services. Trade rules and regulations need to be overhauled to facilitate the circular transition of economies. Addressing the potential trade barriers is key to ensuring the seamless movement of environmental goods and services and the diffusion of circular technologies. There should also be support for businesses in their supply chain management efforts, which may include technical assistance and testing beds for emerging technologies.

Enhanced role of innovation, digitalization, and emerging technologies. Technological solutions and innovations need to be harnessed to accelerate the shift to a circular economy. Blockchain, for example, can provide a means of traceability of material flows and give information on how the product can be recycled or remanufactured. Knowledge tools—such as databases, directory of relevant institutions or experts, and information materials on best practices or technologies—could serve as useful resources for government and industry stakeholders in countries in the nascent stage of their circular journey.

Sustainable finance and innovative investments. With the rapid growth of various forms of sustainable investments, the finance community is critical in encouraging new business models that support the circular economy. However, this entails improving the assessment and governance of climate risks of investments in both linear and circular models. Harmonized sustainability standards are also important to determine the eligibility of initiatives for green funding. In the meantime, governments can drive the shift to circularity by providing subsidies and tax incentives, supporting technological development, and promoting public–private partnerships.

Efficient use of energy and other resources. The sustainable use of energy underlies all economic activities in a circular economy. Therefore, focusing on reducing energy use and adopting renewable sources are vital to promoting a circular economy. Businesses, especially small enterprises, could benefit from capacity-building programs on how to green their production processes as well as monitor and report their carbon performance.

ADB-Supported Circular Initiatives

ADB, through its multidisciplinary approach, identifies circular economy entry points and delivers integrated solutions to its government clients. In particular, ADB is taking a programmatic approach to help communities along the Yangtze River Economic Belt in the People's Republic of China achieve water security and green development and increase their resilience. ADB's multisector support seeks to stimulate the economic development of the Yangtze River Basin while promoting the sustainable use of natural resources in line with the circular economy approach to reduce resource inputs, waste outputs, and pollution.

In addition, ADB is supporting various waste-to-energy (WTE) projects, which help manage the growing volume of urban waste while increasing energy generation from renewable sources. In Viet Nam, ADB is supporting the construction and operation of a series of WTE plants with advanced clean technologies in multiple municipalities. This is the country's first municipal WTE public–private partnership project.

Since the ocean economy represents 20% of the GDP of some Southeast Asian countries, ADB's Promoting Action on Plastic Pollution from Source to Sea aims to address marine plastic pollution and support its member countries as the Global Plastics Treaty is designed and implemented. This ADB technical assistance includes demonstration projects in Indonesia and Viet Nam designed to support the transition to a circular plastics economy and improve waste management, focusing on increasing the quality of recycling and value of plastics. Regional and subregional cross-learning and knowledge sharing are also key project activities.

Recommendations

An integrated systems approach can help ensure a successful transition to a circular economy. The following are recommendations for the consideration of policy makers.

Plan for trade-offs in the policy design process

Policy design and decisions on the circular economy are disrupting established markets, systems, and supply chains, and the outcome's circular nature means that there is far more time for both positive and negative emergent phenomena to manifest. While mitigating measures can be formulated to counter any potential adverse impacts of circular interventions, policy makers need to be agile to manage unforeseen trade-offs. Developing modeling techniques to capture the complexity of our systems is a challenge, but the advances and capabilities of modern technologies offer a major opportunity for understanding circular transitions.

Enact holistic and integrated policies that address opportunities and challenges from both the demand and supply side

The circular transformation calls for holistic policies with a mindset shift and multi-stakeholder collaboration at all levels. Within organizations, interdisciplinary approaches are crucial to the development of circular innovations. Within industries, collaboration on resource optimization can allow one industry to extract value from waste or by-products of another. Moreover, the circular transition is contingent on partnerships between governments and the private sector, which can help identify and finance capital-intensive solutions. Finally, companies need to work with consumers to gain insights into their perceptions and behavior when developing circular solutions.

Develop systems for knowledge sharing and build the capacity of stakeholders

Information sharing is essential for deepening the understanding of this evolving trend. As the library of circular economy transition projects and technological solutions grows, common success factors and areas for improvement can be identified. For businesses and workers, capacity building and reskilling are essential to help them apply circular principles in production processes. Standardized methodologies and tools are also necessary for evaluating their performance and measuring their progress.

Resources

ADB Institute. 2022. *Prospects for Transitioning from a Linear to Circular Economy in Developing Asia*. Tokyo.

ASEAN. 2021. *Framework for Circular Economy for the ASEAN Economic Community*. Jakarta.

Baker, J. 2022. Circular Economy—Systems Thinking: Approaches to Achieve Successful Transitions to a Circular Economy. Presented at the Policy Actions for COVID-19 Economic Recovery Dialogues of the Asian Development Bank. 27 July.

Unlocking the Value of Agrifood Waste Streams

Vandana Dhaul
Chief Operating Officer, ID Capital Pte. Ltd.

Harvesting bananas. After banana harvesting, almost 60% of what is left of the plant is considered waste, but this can be turned into high-value goods, such as fabric and bioethanol (photo by ADB).

Introduction

The agrifood industry generates significant by-products that mostly end up in a landfill or get incinerated. Repurposing these by-products can bring new revenue streams and solutions to environmental and social challenges. Turning banana stems into clothing and making plant-based protein from brewers' spent grain are among the several ways of extracting maximum value from side streams of agrifood production.

In Southeast Asia, which comprises many agrarian-based economies, there is scope to look into the prospects of circularity in agricultural and food waste systems. Shifting from a linear to circular approach in the agrifood industry can deliver economic gains while helping address food security and promote sustainable production and consumption.

Wasted Opportunity

According to the United Nations, food waste is a global issue costing over $2.6 trillion per year, and Southeast Asia is a major contributor. The enormous costs come with a large carbon footprint from methane emitted by rotting food, crop residues, and agricultural by-products. Wastage occurs at various stages of the food chain—production, harvest, sorting, shipping, processing, packaging, wholesale and retail distribution, and consumption. In developed countries like the Republic of Korea and Japan, a significant volume of food is wasted during consumption. In developing economies, food loss happens because of inadequate transportation and storage facilities.

Amid all these challenges, recent disruptive trends highlight several ways to apply circularity in the supply chain. At the agro-industrial level—where most of the opportunities lie for Southeast Asian economies—there is great potential for scaling up circular economy approaches given the relative ease of collecting, storing, and processing of agro-industrial waste, which is relatively homogenous compared with household or retail waste. There is a low risk of contamination, making it easy to ensure food safety. However, valorizing food wastes or converting them into new food products, agricultural inputs, or new materials would depend on local context and demand.

The value potential of side streams can be better understood and analyzed using Bühler's value pyramid (Figure 3.1). At the bottom of the hierarchy, large volumes of food waste can be minimized through prevention and reduction measures, but the value potential for food producers is limited. In contrast, there are more value creation opportunities at the higher end of the pyramid, showing a strong business case for insects as feed and food, and the reuse of waste streams for other new products.

Figure 3.1: Side Stream Valorization Opportunities

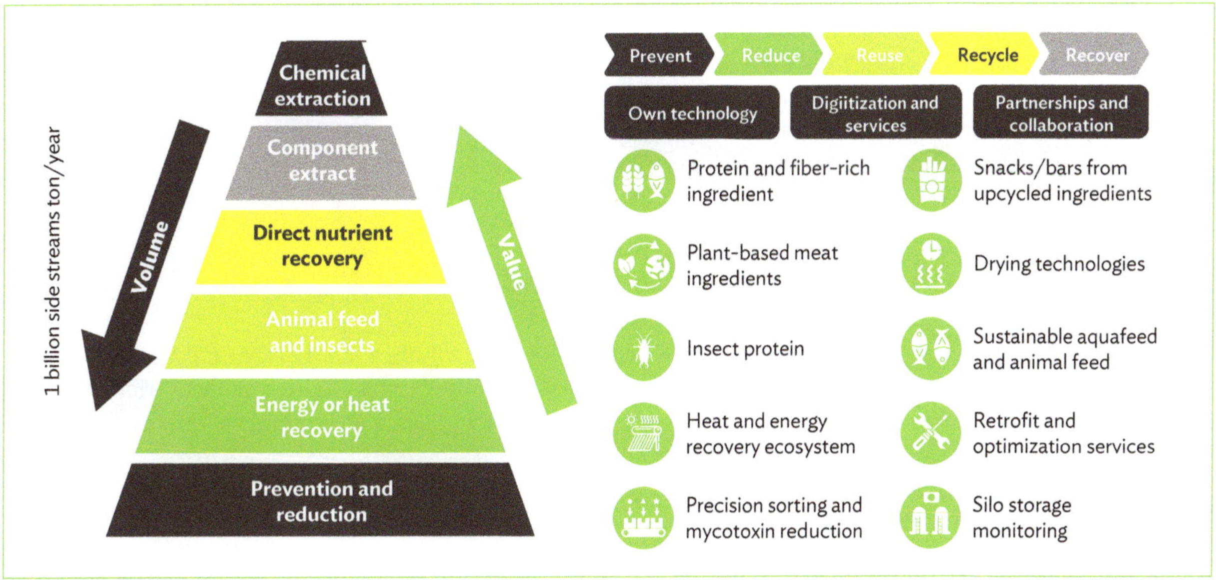

Source: ID Capital Pte Ltd. 2022. *Waste-to-Value: A White Paper on the Future of Food Upcycling in Asia*. Published in partnership with Agency for Science, Technology and Research, Bühler Group, and Dole Sunshine Company as part of the Future Food Asia 2022 Conference. 7 June.

Other important considerations for applying circular economy concepts in agrifood wastes and by-products include the availability of supplies, which may be affected by the seasonality of crops, as well as quality, which can be influenced by climatic conditions and other factors.

Nurturing Circularity in Agrifood

There are several options for reducing waste both upstream and downstream in the agrifood value chain.

Provide tradable credits to encourage food waste reduction

Policy makers can consider designing a carbon credit scheme to incentivize food waste reduction and allow credits to be traded, the proceeds of which drive financing for similar initiatives. To effectively implement this, the government should employ a transparent and understandable methodology for measuring the carbon impact of food rescue.

Support circular initiatives through innovative financing instruments

In addition to tradable credits, sustainable financing solutions can support projects that fight food waste. For example, sustainability-linked bonds are conditional on meeting targets such as reducing food waste and other indicators to lower the environmental footprint. Another example is the World Bank's issuance of sustainable development bonds that mobilized the support of banks, asset managers, insurance companies, and pension funds globally while raising awareness of the need to solve food loss and waste problems.

Promote insect farming for feed and food production

Given the rising feed and food demands across the region, finding sustainable ways to nourish growing populations is imperative. Insect farming shows an inherent ability to convert local organic wastes into useful resources while using minimal resources. This means it is a practical solution that can be applied in the region's low-resource countries. In addition, investments in insects-as-feed solutions, as well as the expansion of the edible insects market, can address hunger and nutrition challenges.

Foster collaboration between companies and farmers

With the infrastructure gaps and prevalence of post-harvest losses in Southeast Asia's developing countries, the private sector has a critical role in supporting agro-processing at the farm level. This collaboration can strengthen market linkages, enabling the agro-processing industry to secure a more stable supply of materials. For farmers, near-farm processing would incentivize the collection, storage, and productive use of agricultural residue and by-products, which could boost their incomes.

Introduce programs to reduce food waste at the consumer level

Behavior change campaigns and policy incentives are crucial to curb the wasteful habits of consumers. In the Republic of Korea, for instance, compulsory food waste recycling using special biodegradable bags has encouraged composting. The fee for these bags covers 60% of the cost of running the scheme, which has increased the amount of food waste recycled (World Economic Forum 2019). Bins are also equipped with radio frequency identification to weigh and charge residents for their waste using an ID card, helping the government save on collection costs. In Japan, national programs were rolled out to retune the next generation's attitude toward food waste. Additionally, a national food bank organization rescues still edible food from grocery stores and other retailers and reallocates it to people in need.

Invest in research and development to explore other valorization opportunities

Governments need to collaborate with universities and institutions and pursue public–private partnerships to research food waste valorization as well as uncover solutions and develop technologies. Singapore is positioning itself as a research and development testing bed for Southeast Asia, a springboard for piloting and then exporting new industrial agrifood waste upcycling technologies and business models. In Thailand, public–private partnerships are central to promoting a bioeconomy that focuses on the sugarcane and cassava sectors.

Waste to Wealth

There are several initiatives and opportunities to produce high-value products from agrifood wastes in Southeast Asia.

In the Philippines, Dole Sunshine Company has partnered with social enterprise Musa Fabric to extract fibers from banana waste. Yarn is woven into fabric and developed into garments. Preventing 4.4 million pieces of banana stems from reaching landfills can reduce approximately 258,720 tons of carbon dioxide equivalent (CO_2e) emissions. Banana waste is instead used to create fashion products worth over $50 million, benefiting the livelihoods of more than a hundred people (Dole Sunshine Company 2022).

Indonesia's palm oil mill effluent—or the liquid waste from palm oil production—can be converted into biogas, a renewable energy source. This could pave the way not only for providing energy to remote rural areas but also for reducing carbon emissions. The country also produces huge volumes of what are known as empty fruit bunches. These are valuable palm oil mill waste by-products that could be used to produce multiple forms of heat, energy, chemicals, feedstocks, and other materials.

Recommendations

The following policy actions are recommended to increase the uptake of circular approaches in the agrifood sector.

Improve data availability on food loss and waste

Sound interventions are hinged on robust data on food loss and waste. It is important to know the sources of food wastes along with their volume and composition to design appropriate measures at each stage of the value chain. This will also help identify food waste streams and strategies for waste recovery.

Raise awareness to increase food valorization initiatives

Many profitable opportunities exist in converting agrifood waste into high-value products, which go untapped because of a lack of awareness of valorization strategies and investment costs. Bringing together industries, governments, and solution providers through knowledge-sharing events will help disseminate the technologies available and valorization options.

Collaborate on circular solutions

Increasing food loss and waste are costing all actors along the food supply chain, including consumers. Therefore, this complex issue requires collaboration at all levels. Farmers, processors, and retailers must work together to counter the factors that lead to losses, such as poor harvesting and processing techniques. At the downstream level, partnering with food rescue programs and working with consumers to influence their behaviors can help reduce waste. Scaling food waste valorization can benefit from public–private collaboration, which can be an effective way of discovering and delivering innovations.

Resources

Aung, M. T. 2021. Bioeconomy in Thailand: At a Glance. *SEI Discussion Brief.* Bangkok: Stockholm Environment Institute.

Broom, D. 2019. South Korea Once Recycled 2% of Its Food Waste. Now It Recycles 95%. World Economic Forum. 12 April.

Dhaul, V. 2022 Agrifood Waste Upcycling Opportunities in Asia-Pacific. Presented at the Policy Actions for COVID-19 Economic Recovery Dialogues of the Asian Development Bank. 27 July.

Dole Sunshine Company. Dole Sunshine Company Turns Banana Waste into Fibres of Purpose with Musa Fabric.

Future Food Asia. 2022. *Waste-to-Value: Future of Food Upcycling in Asia.* Singapore. 7 June.

About the PACER Dialogues

Policy Actions for COVID-19 Economic Recovery (PACER) Dialogues, supported by the Asian Development Bank (ADB) under the BIMP-EAGA, IMT-GT, and GMS Capacity Building Program (B-I-G Program), explore measures that can help B-I-G member countries, Singapore, and Timor-Leste bounce back from the COVID-19 pandemic and accelerate economic recovery.

Overcoming COVID-19 Together

At a Special ASEAN Summit on COVID-19 on 14 April 2020, leaders called on ASEAN to "act jointly and decisively to control the spread of the disease while mitigating its adverse impact on our people's livelihood, our societies, and economies." Leaders also called for sharing best practices between member states and external partners to respond to COVID-19 effectively. Consistent with this call for action, the B-I-G Program convened the PACER Dialogues to share cutting-edge knowledge and best practices and explore means of strengthening cooperation to mitigate the devastating effects of COVID-19.

Sharing Approaches and Lessons to Accelerate COVID-19 Recovery

Countries in the region and across the world are grappling with balancing policy responses that can mitigate the economic costs of the COVID-19 crisis while also minimizing risks to society. The PACER Dialogues shared global, regional, and country-level good practices and lessons that can provide countries with new ideas and actionable insights as they lay the groundwork for medium- and long-term economic recovery. Sharing knowledge and learning from others allow countries to explore a broader range of policy options as they tailor recovery and resilient measures to the unique context of their respective nations.

Objectives

PACER Dialogues objectives included

- enhancing awareness of policy issues and actions that can facilitate economic recovery and resilience;
- sharing knowledge, lessons, and experiences on COVID-19 recovery and resilience strategies, policies, and plans;
- exploring collaborative responses and coordinated actions geared toward increased resilience, preparedness, and effective recovery; and
- strengthening connections between policy makers, development planners, and relevant stakeholders tasked with spearheading the COVID-19 crisis recovery and resilience.

Format, Process, and Policy Briefs

A series of 90-minute PACER Dialogues were held from June 2020 to July 2022. The dialogue process includes (i) moderators' introduction, (ii) experts' presentation, (iii) reactions from panel discussants, (iv) open discussion with questions and inputs by participating government officials, and (v) moderator synthesis or summary.

The PACER Dialogues are organized to help decision makers broaden their perspectives, appreciate the wider implications of critical policy choices, and identify concrete policy actions. Background papers are provided in advance to facilitate informed discussions. Policy briefs for each dialogue are produced as knowledge products (outputs) and shared on ADB's knowledge platform, Development Asia.

Themes and Topics

Topics of the PACER Dialogues have three main categories: (i) overarching strategic approaches for forging national strategies for COVID-19 economic recovery, (ii) cross-cutting thematic and sector-specific approaches to facilitate economic recovery and resilience and mitigate the devastating effects of COVID-19, and (iii) regional cooperation responses to COVID-19 to complement national strategies.

- Overarching strategic approaches for national recovery includes economic and financial measures to tackle COVID-19; good practices in designing, financing, and implementing plans for bouncing back from COVID-19; employing big data and digital technology to enhance COVID-19 responses; and mobilizing finance in the wake of COVID-19.

- Crosscutting thematic and sector approaches include providing health measures to enhance resilience to pandemics, interventions for economic reopenings, and readiness for vaccine distribution; supporting small and medium-sized enterprises and start-ups to mitigate the negative effects of the crisis; developing effective social protection responses; helping the tourism industry bounce back from COVID-19; harnessing digital technology for education; and transforming TVET systems for greater resilience.

- Regional cooperation responses to complement national strategies and emphasize public goods are also explored, such as multisector interventions in health, tourism, migration, food security, trade and e-commerce, energy transition, and green recovery.

Experts

Select ADB staff, government officials, academicians, private sector experts, and development partners were invited to serve as presenters and discussants.

Participants and Audience

Policy makers and planners involved in the various policy domains of the COVID-19 crisis recovery and resilience, especially from the ministries of finance and the BIMP-EAGA, IMT-GT, and GMS national secretariats, served as core participants. Depending on the themes and topics, participation was extended to other ministries, the private sector, academe, civil society, and international organizations.

A total of 1,279 participants from ASEAN member countries, the People's Republic of China, and Timor-Leste, including representatives from development partners, attended the 19 PACER Dialogues—1,084 participants were government officials from BIMP-EAGA, IMT-GT, and GMS with 541 (42%) women, and the majority (738, 58%) were at the director level and above.

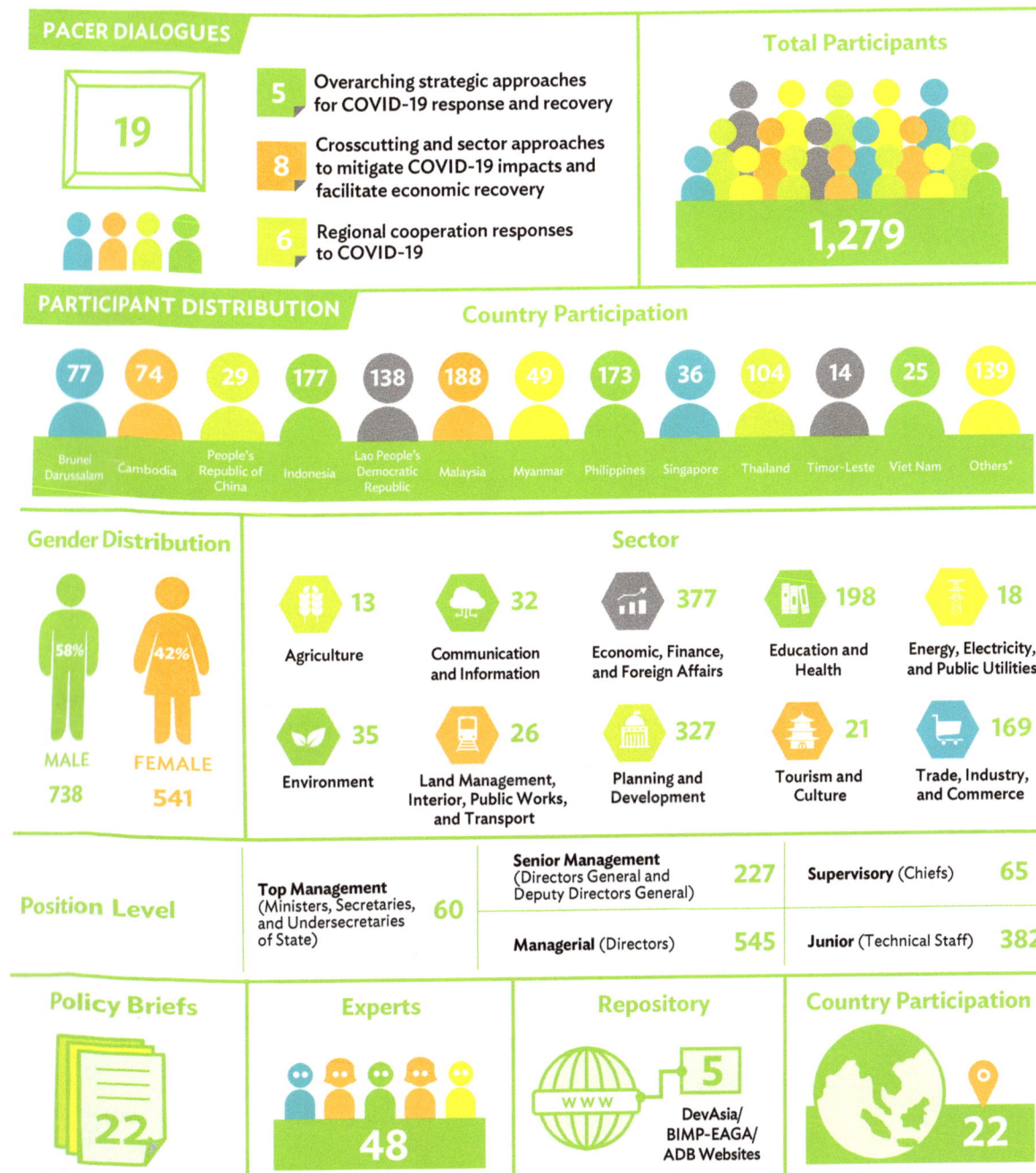

PACER DIALOGUES

19

- **5** Overarching strategic approaches for COVID-19 response and recovery
- **8** Crosscutting and sector approaches to mitigate COVID-19 impacts and facilitate economic recovery
- **6** Regional cooperation responses to COVID-19

Total Participants
1,279

PARTICIPANT DISTRIBUTION

Country Participation

Brunei Darussalam	Cambodia	People's Republic of China	Indonesia	Lao People's Democratic Republic	Malaysia	Myanmar	Philippines	Singapore	Thailand	Timor-Leste	Viet Nam	Others*
77	74	29	177	138	188	49	173	36	104	14	25	139

Gender Distribution
MALE 58% — 738
FEMALE 42% — 541

Sector
- Agriculture 13
- Communication and Information 32
- Economic, Finance, and Foreign Affairs 377
- Education and Health 198
- Energy, Electricity, and Public Utilities 18
- Environment 35
- Land Management, Interior, Public Works, and Transport 26
- Planning and Development 327
- Tourism and Culture 21
- Trade, Industry, and Commerce 169

Position Level
- Top Management (Ministers, Secretaries, and Undersecretaries of State) 60
- Senior Management (Directors General and Deputy Directors General) 227
- Supervisory (Chiefs) 65
- Managerial (Directors) 545
- Junior (Technical Staff) 382

Policy Briefs 22
Experts 48
Repository 5 — DevAsia/BIMP-EAGA/ADB Websites
Country Participation 22

ADB = Asian Development Bank, BIMP EAGA = Brunei Darussalam-Indonesia-Malaysia-Philippines East ASEAN Growth Area, COVID-19 = coronavirus disease, PACER = Policy Actions for COVID-19 Economic Recovery.
* Representatives from private sector and nonprofit organizations, ADB, and development partners.
Source: ADB.

Invitation, Dissemination, and Repository

The policy dialogues were by invitation and coursed through the BIMP-EAGA and IMT-GT senior officials, GMS national coordinators, and finance ministries. Background papers were provided in advance to facilitate informed discussions. A public repository summarizing PACER Dialogues (without attribution) was hosted on ADB's knowledge platform, Development Asia.

List of PACER Dialogues, 2020–2022

No.	Date	Title/Theme	Experts	Policy Brief/s
1	3 Jun 2020	Tackling COVID-19: Economic and Financial Measures of the Republic of Korea	• Kwangchul Ji Director of International Financial Institutions Division, Ministry of Economy and Finance, Republic of Korea	• Policy Lessons from a Pandemic: The Korean Experience
2	17 Jun 2020	Experience and Lessons of New Zealand in responding to COVID-19	• Mark Blackmore Senior Representative for Singapore, India, and Southeast Asia, New Zealand Treasury • Mario Di Maio Principal Advisor, New Zealand Treasury	• Lessons We Can Learn from New Zealand's COVID-19 Strategy
3	24 Jun 2020	Tourism: Respond, Restart, and Recover	• Tiffany Misrahi Vice President of Policy, World Travel and Tourism Council • Mario Hardy Chief Executive Officer, Pacific Asia Travel Association • Jens Thraenhart Executive Director, Mekong Tourism Coordinating Office	• Policy Options to Accelerate Travel and Tourism Recovery in Southeast Asia
4	1 Jul 2020	Minimum Public Health Interventions for Post COVID-19 Lockdown: Lives and Livelihoods	• Jeremy Lim Co-Director of Global Health, Saw Swee Hock School of Public Health, National University of Singapore	• Harmonizing Health Standards for Post-Quarantine COVID-19 Settings
5	8 Jul 2020	Bouncing Back Support to SMEs for COVID-19 Recovery	• Paul Vandenberg Principal Economist, Economic Research and Development Impact Department, Asian Development Bank • Foo Ngee Kee Co-Founder and President of the SME Association of Sabah	• How SMEs Can Bounce Back from the COVID-19 Crisis

continued on the next page

Table continued

No.	Date	Title/Theme	Experts	Policy Brief/s
6	15 Jul 2020	Migration and Health: Implications of COVID-19 and Achieving Universal Health Coverage	• Patrick Duigan Regional Migration Health Advisor for Asia and the Pacific, International Organization for Migration • Jadej Thammatcharee Deputy Secretary-General, National Health Security Office, Thailand • Heather Canon Vice President for Capacity Building, ELEVATE	• Coming Out Stronger from COVID-19: Policy Options on Migrant Health and Immigration
7	22 Jul 2020	Harnessing Digital Technologies for Education amid COVID-19	• Ashish Dhawan Founder and Chair, Central Square Foundation • Chad Pasha Head of Asia Pacific for Global Government Partnerships, Coursera	• An Equity-focused Digital Strategy for Education during and after COVID-19 • Policy Lessons from Coursera: Mitigating Education Disruptions and Job Loss
8	4 Aug 2020	Post-COVID-19 New Normal: Implications for Startup Ecosystems	• Stephan Kuester Head, Global Ecosystem Strategy, Startup Genome • Seow Hui Lim Director, Startup Development, Innovation and Enterprise Group, Enterprise Singapore • Christiaan Kaptein Partner, Integra Partners	• Fostering Resilient Startup Ecosystems in the New Normal
9	12 Aug 2020	Accelerating Digital Financial Services and Infrastructure	• David Lee Kuo Chuen Professor, Singapore University of Social Sciences • Haerok Ko General Manager, Korea Financial Telecommunications and Clearings Institute	• Building the Infrastructure for Digital Finance during COVID-19 and Beyond
10	19 Aug 2020	Enhancing Readiness for Large-Scale Vaccine Distribution amid COVID-19	• Farzana Muhib Asia Team Lead for Vaccine Implementation, PATH • Hannah Kettler Director for Financing and Partnerships, PATH's Center for Vaccines Innovation and Access • Huong Minh Vu Regional Technical Advisor for Vaccine Implementation, PATH	• Enhancing Readiness for Large-Scale Distribution of the COVID-19 Vaccine
11	26 Aug 2020	Social Protection Interventions as Medium- and Long-Term Responses amid COVID-19 and Beyond	• Valentina Barca Independent Social Protection Expert • Edward Archibald Independent Social Protection Expert	• Social Protection Interventions as Medium- and Long-Term Responses to the Pandemic

continued on the next page

Table continued

No.	Date	Title/Theme	Experts	Policy Brief/s
12	23 Sep 2020	Adaptive Control of COVID-19 Outbreaks: Policy Approaches	• Anup Malani Professor, University of Chicago	• Adaptive Control of COVID-19 Outbreaks: Policy Approaches
13	24 Feb 2021	Managing safe, equitable, and effective COVID-19 vaccination	• Kwangchul Ji Director of International Financial Institutions Division, Ministry of Economy and Finance, Republic of Korea • Teodoro Padilla Executive Director Pharmaceutical and Healthcare Association of the Philippines • Eduardo Banzon Principal Health Specialist, Sectors Group, Asian Development Bank	• Managing Safe, Equitable, and Effective COVID-19 Vaccination
14	10 Jun 2021	Future of Skills Development in the time of COVID-19	• Sameer Khatiwada Senior Public Management Economist, Sectors Group, Asian Development Bank • Rosanna Urdaneta Deputy Director General, Technical Education and Skills Development Authority (TESDA) • Srinivas Reddy Branch Chief, Skills and Employability Branch, International Labour Organization • Michael Fung Deputy Chief Executive (Industry), Chief Human Resource Officer, and Chief Data Officer, SkillsFuture Singapore	• The Future of Skills Development in the Time of COVID-19
15	8 Jul 2021	Green Policies for Post-COVID-19 Economic Recovery	• Anouj Mehta Country Director of Thailand Resident Mission, Asian Development Bank • Paola Sherina Alvarez Assistant Secretary for International Finance and Special Projects Department of Finance (Philippines) • Paroche Hutachareon Senior Expert on Bond Market Development, Public Debt Management Office, Ministry of Finance (Thailand)	• Green Policies for Post-COVID-19 Economic Recovery in Southeast Asia

continued on the next page

Table continued

No.	Date	Title/Theme	Experts	Policy Brief/s
16	3 Aug 2021	Digitizing trade in the new normal	• Oswald Kulyer Digital Standards Initiative Managing Director, International Chamber of Commerce (ICC) • Luca Castellani Legal Officer, United Nations Commission on International Trade Law (UNCITRAL) • Sin Yong Loh Director for Trade, Infocomm Media Development Authority of Singapore (IMDA) • Kobsak Duangdee Secretary General, Thai Bankers' Association (TBA)	• Enabling the Digital Transformation of Global Trade in the New Normal
17	28 Sep 2021	Accelerating e-commerce in the new normal	• Le The Phuc Ministry of Industry and Trade, Viet Nam • Satvinder Singh Deputy Secretary-General, Association of Southeast Asian Nations (ASEAN) • Mario Masaya Digital Policy Director, US–ASEAN Business Council	• Forging a Path to Recovery through E-Commerce • Accelerating E-Commerce in ASEAN
18	20 Apr 2022	Accelerating Clean Energy Transition in the New Normal	• Pradeep Tharakan Director, Energy Transition, Sectors Group, Asian Development Bank • Paola Sherina Alvarez Assistant Secretary for International Finance and Special Projects, Department of Finance (Philippines) • Andriah Feby Misna Director of Various New and Renewable Energy at the Ministry of Energy and Mineral Resources (Indonesia) • Anh Tuan Nguyen Energy Policies and Energy Sector Institutional and Regulatory Framework Expert, EU–Viet Nam Sustainable Energy Transition Facility (EVSETF)	• Powering the Clean Energy Transition
19	27 Jul 2022	Transitioning from a linear to circular economy in post-pandemic Southeast Asia	• James Baker Senior Circular Economy Specialist (Plastic Wastes), Climate Change and Sustainable Development Department, Asian Development Bank • Latifahaida Abdul Latif Head of Analysis and Monitoring on Finance and Socioeconomic Issues Division, ASEAN Secretariat • Vandana Dhaul Chief Operating Officer, ID Capital Pte. Ltd.	• A Systems Approach for Transitioning Southeast Asia to a Circular Economy • Unlocking the Value of Agrifood Waste Streams

About the B-I-G Program

The Brunei Darussalam–Indonesia–Malaysia–Philippines East ASEAN Growth Area (BIMP-EAGA), the Indonesia–Malaysia–Thailand Growth Triangle (IMT-GT), and the Greater Mekong Subregion (GMS) Capacity Building Program, or B-I-G Program, is a regional capacity development initiative for government officials to enhance capacities in developing policies, programs, and projects that support physical, institutional, and people-to-people connectivity in Southeast Asia and the People's Republic of China. The B-I-G Program provides opportunities for knowledge and experience sharing and networking among the three subregional programs, given their unique roles as building blocks for Asian integration. It is funded by the Asian Development Bank (ADB) and the governments of the Republic of Korea and the People's Republic of China.

B-I-G Program Team

ALFREDO PERDIGUERO
Regional Head, Regional Cooperation and Integration, Southeast Asia Department
Asian Development Bank

JASON RUSH
Principal Regional Cooperation Specialist

CAMILLE GENEVIEVE M. SALVADOR
Senior Operations Assistant

PAMELA ASIS-LAYUGAN
Institutional and Capacity Development Specialist (International Consultant)

JORDANA QUEDDENG-COSME
Regional Development Analyst (National Consultant)

ALONA MAE H. AGUSTIN
Regional Development Analyst (National Consultant)

6 ADB Avenue, Mandaluyong City
1550 Metro Manila, Philippines
www.bigconnectivity.org

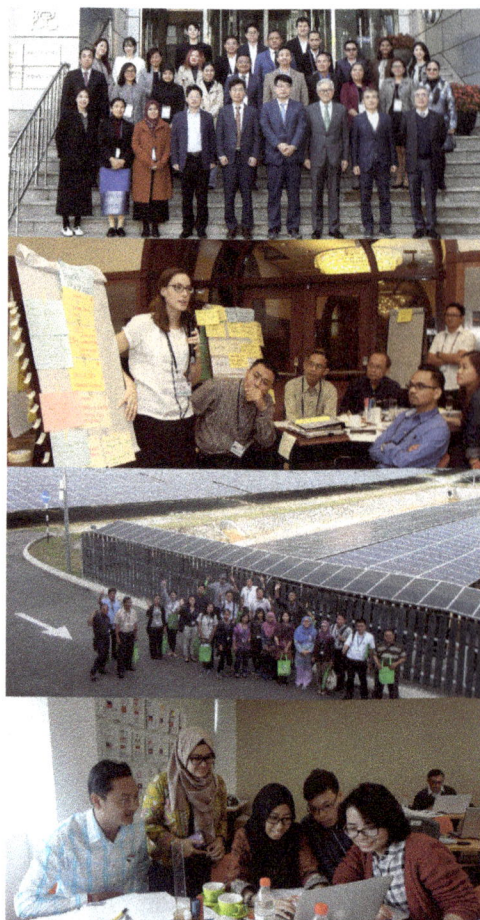

www.ingramcontent.com/pod-product-compliance
Lightning Source LLC
Chambersburg PA
CBHW050050220326
41599CB00045B/7353